The Second and Third Nine Lives of Squeekie the Bookstore Cat

SQUEEKIE THE BOOKSTORE CAT

with help from his very talented Friends

Copyright © 2017 Squeekie the Bookstore Cat

Second Edition Copyright © 2019

All rights reserved.

ISBN: 978-1-7331837-1-0

DEDICATION

For my first Person, for being able to give me up to a bookstore where I can be loved and given attention all day long.

And to all cats who are still looking for their forever home.

CONTENTS

	Acknowledgements	i
1.	Squeekie Saves the Store *Natalie J. Damschroder*	1
2.	Copy Cat *Molly Lemke*	9
3.	Squeekie vs. the Stinkie Apocalypse *Jay Smith*	21
4.	Hide and Go Squeek *Eric Hardenbrook*	39
5.	Everybody Needs a Friend *Carrie Jacobs*	47
6.	Squeekie and the Mermaid *Lynne Reeder*	57
7.	Squeekie in Mageia *Kiera Lehman*	65
8.	Squeekie and Abbey *Stella Phillips*	75
9.	The Battle of the Bookstore *Hannah Chapman*	83
10.	Squeekie Cat Detective *Lindsay Grubb*	95

11. Squeekie and the Nine Lives   103
   Donna Leiss

12. Squeekie's Big (Imaginary) Night   111
   Joshua Short

13. Squeekie and the Goddess   117
   Jennifer Woodings

14. The Drunken Comic Book Monkeys vs. Squeekie   127
   Brian Koscienski & Chris Pisano

15. A Friends Like Squeekie   135
   Melissa Ford

16. The Tenth Life of Squeekie the Bookstore Cat   141
   Beth Ann Hargraves

17. The Way of the Beloved Kitty   153
   Heidi Hormel

18. Tiny Mighty Heroes   163
   Teddy Maurer

   Squeekie's Appearance Rider   173
   Jay Smith

ACKNOWLEDGMENTS

I would like to thank everyone who submitted a story for this collection. Thank you for understanding and sharing the gift that is me, Squeekie.

1

Squeekie Saves the Store

Natalie J. Damschroder

"Night, Squeekie. See you in the morning!"

The lock snicked and the door rattled as the human tested it. Feet crunched as they walked away, and Squeekie's ears flicked, listening for the rumble that meant they weren't coming back inside for something they forgot. Then that, too, faded, and all was silent.

And Squeekie went to work. He padded silently down the last row of bookstacks, ensuring all was in its place, peaceful. He was Adventure Cat, on the prowl, prepared to defend and protect. Down the back wall, with a pause to nod at Bob the Bookstore Ghost, out for a stroll. Or a glide, since his feet didn't move.

He was halfway up the first row when the door rattled. He froze, concentrating. Scraping noises came from the front of the store, and a harsh voice, muffled too much to understand the words, reached his ears.

He scrambled—no, *dashed* to the front of the store and up the best route to the top of the shelves next to the counter, where he could see whoever was coming in but could hide in the shadows. The voices were clearer now, using the kinds of words and tone he rarely heard in the store. These were men, angry men, and they did not belong here.

The door opened. With a scuffle, two men came in. They wore what the no-longer-small human called hoodies, so Squeekie couldn't see their faces. He had never seen—or smelled—them before. A strange odor tickled his nose, and he pawed it to keep from sneezing and giving away his position. He had the advantage, the high ground, like the Navy SEALs in those books, and he wasn't giving way.

"Hurry and get away from the door!" one of the men said. The other one turned the lock and they backed hurriedly out of the foyer. They stood, watching the entrance, panting like stupid dogs for a few seconds. In the cage next to them, the two young cats (Squeekie forgot their names, since they'd only been here two days and he never bothered to learn them for at least a week) stood and meowed. One purred, the attention hog, and the shorter guy flipped back his hood and leaned down, smiling, the light from the parking lot showing broken teeth.

"Hey, little one. Ain't you just the cutest."

"Leave it alone." The bigger guy shoved past him and turned, tapping his thumb and pinky against his thigh, back and forth, back and forth, really fast, Squeekie could catch it, could pounce and stop it...

He was crouching. He shook off the instinct and settled into a low stance, as if he'd meant to shift his position all along.

Short Guy straightened, the smile going away. "How long you think we gotta wait?"

"A while. Maybe morning."

No way. Squeekie knew these guys were bad. It was instinct, which, as Adventure Cat, he had more of than the usual kitty. They reeked of desperation, like a lot of the cats did when they came in here from really bad places. Those cats got love and food and protection and found good homes. These men would just get more desperate. And that meant if Squeekie's humans showed up in the morning, *this* could become a bad place.

Big Guy eyed the space behind the counter, then walked around the favorites rack and over to the button machine. "Think they keep money in here overnight?"

Short Guy didn't answer, and Big Guy started pushing buttons. Squeekie had to stop him. Mother was always in a really bad mood if anything happened with the green paper. He had to stop Big Guy. He yowled and leaped, landing on his head, claws digging in to the hoodie and the scalp beneath.

Squeekie Saves the Store

He had really good claws.

The man screamed and spun. Squeekie held on as he staggered around, knocking over stacks of books. Big Guy finally got his hands around Squeekie's middle and flung him off. Squeekie hit the ground running, streaking around the corner well ahead of the clunky, thunking boots behind him.

"Get that cat!" Big Guy yelled, but Squeekie ducked under a shelf and stilled.

"Where is he?" the man bellowed.

"Where's who?" Short Guy asked, as if he hadn't seen what just happened.

Squeekie stifled a purr of satisfaction. These guys were dumb. This would be easy. He stayed where he was, letting the men stomp around looking for him for a few minutes.

Eventually, Short Guy said, "I gotta take a leak."

Squeekie knew what that meant. He slunk out of his hiding spot and glided behind the shelves to the back of the store, while Short Guy stomped around some more, looking for the room with the whirlpool fountain. When he found it and slammed the door, Squeekie made his move. Next to the door was a tall rack of paperback books. He knew just the right angle to knock it over. He'd done it before. This time would be on purpose.

In a few leaps he was on top of a tall shelf. He wiggled his feet under himself just right, stared at the place he needed to land, and jumped. All four feet hit the rack, his momentum—he loved that word, just like the Human Who Writes Funny Books did—taking him and the rack to the floor, right in front of the door. He was flying off the rack before it hit the ground, landing softly and spinning to check if it was going to work. Short Guy yelled something from inside the room. Seconds passed. The whirlpool fountain made its water noise, and then he tried to open the door. It stuck. The man yelled again and pushed harder. The rack moved, but came up against one of the heavy wooden chairs from the craft table and stopped.

"Halp!" Short Guy bellowed through the crack.

"Shut *up!*" Big Guy yelled back from the front of the store, but didn't seem to be walking this way. "You want someone to hear us?"

Short Guy grumbled and tried to squeeze through the gap, but it was too small.

Okay, phase one was complete. Now Squeekie needed a way to make sure these guys didn't want to stay here. He'd already made it unpleasant. Now he needed to make it scarier than going outside was for them. And he knew just what to do.

Not all the ghosts in the store were friendly ones.

He ran past Big Guy into the back room and toward the stairs. Big Guy yelled "hey!" and started after him. Squeekie stopped until he got around the corner and could see him, then ran again. His heart thundered. Taunting the thing in the basement was scary for him, too, but he was brave, a defender, a protector, and he could handle what was coming. He halted at the top of the stairs, listening to the footsteps behind him, feeling their vibration, and when Big Guy was close enough, he gave a mournful howl that echoed into the darkness beneath. He waited, his whole body tense, knowing those big hands would close around him any second.

C'mon, c'mon, you always come for that cry. He used to taunt the Being from Below until that one time he stayed too long and the ghost's tentacles had caught him. He never wanted to feel that sorrow and despair again. But if he timed this right…

There.

He twisted to the side, feet scrabbling on the concrete floor until they got traction—another good word, he liked words related to his physical skills—and got out of the way just before the tentacles waved up out of the gloom.

Big Guy shrieked and pinwheeled his arms, trying to stop and back up at the same time. He fell on his butt and pushed with his feet, looking like a big bug, as the ghost groped for him. He screamed again, and from the other room, Short Guy shouted, too, his voice afraid. Finally Big Guy got his feet under him—slower and clumsier than a dog, even, a cat would have been much more graceful and fast—and ran back out into the main part of the store. Squeekie followed him all the way to the back.

"What? What? What happened? Are you all right? What's going on? Is it the cops?" Short Guy was wedged into the gap, one foot and one arm through, but stuck at the shoulder and lower leg.

Big Guy bent to grab the rack and heave it out of the way, and Short Guy tumbled out onto his hands and knees.

"We gotta get out of here."

"What about the cops?"

"I'd rather go to jail than spend another minute in here with that *thing.*" He hauled his friend up by the back of his hoodie.

Short Guy squinted at Squeekie. "What thing, the cat?"

Squeekie tilted his head, and Short Guy smiled at him.

"Aw, he's cute, too. Not as cute at the little one, but—"

"Shut up." Big Guy slapped Short Guy on the back of the head and herded him toward the front door. "Not him. Devil cat," he grumbled, and muttered more things under his breath.

Once again Squeekie followed them until they reached the door. He sat in the foyer archway, watching them, tail swishing against the floor. They peered out, looking nervous.

"Maybe we should wait," Short Guy suggested.

Big Guy looked back at Squeekie. He stared back. He always won staring contests, unless he got bored, and even then he won, because it was a decision, not a have to, when he looked away. This time he wasn't looking away. It didn't take long. Big Guy shook his head. "No. We leave now." He pushed the door open, and they went outside.

Blue and red lights flashed, and a short, loud *"whoooop"* sounded. Both guys threw their hands up in the air. Then they stepped forward, out of Squeekie's sight.

His job here was done.

Anika padded up to him, blinking sleepily. "What are you doing out here, Squeekie? So much noise. You interrupted my beauty nap."

"Nothing you have to worry about."

She licked her paw a couple of times. "Good. Now get me some treats." She turned and strolled away.

Squeekie waited long enough to show Anika that she wasn't the boss of him, and then he went to knock over and gnaw open the tub. He deserved a few treats, himself.

The next morning, he was basking in a sunbeam when his people arrived. He flicked the tip of his tail to say hello and absorbed their pats of greeting, but didn't leave his comfy spot.

"I can't believe it!" Mother's friend said. "I'm so glad you weren't here! They could have—" She cleared her throat and looked at Mother's young person.

Mother shrugged. "It was the middle of the night. We didn't even hear the phone when they tried to call to tell us. I have to look around to see if anything is missing. The door was unlocked all night. But get this. They said one of the guys was hysterical, yelling about a demon cat and a murdering ghost." She reached over to stroke Squeekie. "They're talking about you, aren't they, you clever thing?"

He yawned. It was all in a night's work for Adventure Cat.

AUTHOR BIOGRAPHY

Natalie J. Damschroder is a multi-published author of contemporary and paranormal romance, with an emphasis on romantic adventure. She also writes YA paranormal adventure as NJ Damschroder. A 2012 recipient of the RWA Service Award and two-time finalist in the EPIC eBook Awards romantic suspense category, she is also a multi-finalist in the International Digital Awards, and the third book in her Goddesses Rising trilogy, *Sunroper*, won the 2014 Prism for Light Paranormal Romance.

Natalie grew up in Massachusetts and loves the New England Patriots more than anything. (Except her family. And writing and reading. And popcorn.) When she's not writing, revising, proofreading, or promoting her work, she works as a freelance project manager. She and her husband have two daughters, one of whom is also a novelist. (The other one prefers math. Smart kid. Practical.) You can learn more about her at www.nataliedamschroder.com or www.njdamschroder.com, where you'll also find links to her blogs and social media.

2

Copy Cat

Molly Lemke

It is a quiet night at Cupboard Maker Books. A full moon peers in through the shop's doorway, making mysteries out of tattered spines and shelves with its silvery light. It makes a ghost out of Squeekie the bookstore cat, whose Siamese coat becomes fringed with moonlight, and whose eyes become lamps to whoever glances in. Then he blinks, and they are normal again – blue, and slightly crossed.

This is not necessarily Squeekie's favorite time of the day. Sure, he gets to rearrange his fur without anyone petting it back into chaos again. He gets to do whatever he wants without any hollers of "Stop it, Squeekie!" Climb the bookshelves like a ninja? Eat the receipt paper and spit it up on Michelle's chair? Ride a book like a sled down the Yellow Brick Road painted on the bookshop floor? Yes, he can do all these things. But on the flip side, there's nobody around to obey his wishes or admire him, either. He's tried with the Castaway Kittens; adoptable cats that rotate in and out of the shop. At best, they giggle and scamper away into the stacks. At worst, they cross their eyes mockingly at him and try to bite his tail.

Then, too, are the mysterious nighttime events.

The first was on a full moon night (just like this one, come to think of it). He was lounging next to the entrance door (again, just like tonight) and watching the trains pass by in the darkness. At first, there was a tickle on his ear. Then came a whispering and rustling from behind him. *Kittens!* he thought. *Trying to sneak up on me!* Well, Squeekie hadn't been born yesterday. He began to lick a leg, waiting for them to appear out of the corner of his eye.

"HALT, knave!" a voice said from nearby.

Squeekie whirled onto his hind feet and flailed into the darkness like a boxer. "Nice try, kittens!" he yowled. "Now take that! And that! And...that?" There wasn't anything there. Something flashed near his right foot, and he let out a squawk and stumbled backwards at a sudden stabbing pain.

A mouse, of all things, advanced on him, brandishing a knitting needle. "What have you done with the princess? Tell me, beast! Or feel my sword again," it warned.

Squeekie stared at the mouse in outrage. "Get that thing away from me," he said. As a bookstore cat, Squeekie had seen a lot of strange things. More to the point, he had put up with a lot of strange things, and darned if he was going to let some overdressed rodent be the one that cracked him. Undeterred, the mouse advanced, still blithering on about princesses.

The next morning, Squeekie was awoken from a sound sleep by a yelp. "Who put this here??" Jason said, waving the knitting needle that he had just pried from his sole. "Squeekie!" He picked up the book – *The Tale of Desperaux* – that lay, fallen open, on the floor, next to where the offending object had been found. "You need to be more careful, mister."

Squeekie yawned and closed his eyes again. He lived with a horde of kittens; he was used to being the scapecat. Besides, he had a mouse meal to sleep off.

The incidents only became more ridiculous as the month wore on. One night, he startled a little girl in the stacks who was sitting cross-legged on the floor with a book. He'd only wanted to say hi, but when he found himself suddenly levitating in the air in front of her face, he did what any surprised cat would do – hollered and scratched her on the nose. She fell backwards into the shelves and vanished (and knocked down a slew of books, another mess that was put on his head on the morning).

Another time, he found the Castaways had cornered a pigeon below the Emerald City. "Do you have any cookies?!" the pigeon yelled at Squeekie when he came into view. "I WANT A COOKIE!"

Copy Cat

One of the kittens leaped at the bird, outstretched paw dislodging only a feather as it flapped onto a higher shelf. Squeekie watched for a moment, then went to take a nap as far away from the scene as possible.

After a month spent chasing after deranged animals, witches and wizards, pirates, child detectives, adult detectives, werewolves, and everything else under the sun, Squeekie is sick of this nonsense. Little does he know, however, that the worst is yet to come.

Tonight – this calm, full-moon night – he has big plans. He is going to ignore whichever hobgoblin appears from the books, because he has better things to do. Annika, fellow bookstore cat, has divined the newest location of the hidden treat stash, but isn't strong enough to break into the cabinet.

Leave it to me, thinks Squeekie; not that he plans on sharing or anything.

As he crosses the light-dappled floor to the cabinet in question, his ears flick at the sound of a familiar, rustling whisper. *Ugh. Ignore it, ignore it.* There is a slight problem. The trove of treats is behind the counter. Unusually, the rustling comes from atop the counter, directly in Squeekie's way. What books do they keep up there? It looks as though he will have to deal with it after all. Hopefully it is another easy fix, like that fat toad with the car; he'd planted his paw on the hood and watched as the amphibian tried to accelerate, honked the horn desperately, and finally tumbled from the driver's seat and lolloped away into the maze of bookshelves, not to be seen again.

Thing is, the rustling sounds different tonight. There is a hint of nails itching on chalkboards. It sounds...squeaky.

He steps back in alarm as one of *his* books, *The First Nine Lives of Squeekie the Bookstore Cat*, tumbles off the counter. It bounces, then lands with pages sprawled open. A paw reaches up from within the book. Another paw joins it, then another, until a cat steps up from inside the book and stands with all fours atop the Yellow Brick Road. Its head swivels, and familiar blue eyes gaze into his own.

"No," gasps Squeekie.

"Yes!" someone says – not the doppelSqueekie. A Castaway Kitten comes galloping out of the shelves, ready with another contrary retort to Squeekie's next words. She skids to a halt when she sees the "stranger," eyes round as tea saucers. "Who are YOU?" she says, and skitters forward to give the doppelSqueekie a sniff.

The cat purrs. "I'm Squeekie, the Bookstore Cat. And who are you?" The kitten opens her mouth, but the original Squeekie butts in with a growl.

"No, you're not! There's only one Squeekie here, and that's me."

The kitten arches her back protectively in front of the doppelSqueekie. More little faces are popping out of the woodwork; more kittens coming to surround the new cat, who licks each kitten's head like it knows who they are and approves. "Hey," the first kitten protests. "Don't be mean. You ain't never even asked me what my name is, and I've lived here two months."

That's true. During his time as the bookstore cat, so many kittens and cats have come and gone that he has stopped bothering to learn their names. It's not something he's proud of, so he tries to cover: "Of course I have." Squeekie eyeballs the kitten's black coat. "You're Midnight," he says with false confidence.

"Lucky guess!" The Castaways are beginning to murmur amongst themselves. Midnight puffs up even more, a Halloween cat in training. "We're thinkin'," she says, "we're thinkin' that we like this new Squeekie. He's nice, and he wants to know what our names are. But," the murmuring grows louder, "we can't have *two* Squeekies. You hear what I'm sayin'?"

Squeekie is still trying to puzzle out this turn of events when she opens her pink mouth wide, showing tiny white fangs: "GET 'IM!"

To his utter astonishment, a tide of kittens floods his way. His brain reacts before he can even catch up, turning tail and running from the swarm of nipping mouths and pricking claws. They chase him down the Yellow Brick Road, up and down the aisles, across the counter, and finally, up the catwalks and into the rafters. He clings to a beam, panting, as the kittens boo and hiss at him in a cluster on the catwalk ramp. "And stay there!" an orange tabby sniffs, before they all sashay back down to ground level, surrounding the doppelSqueekie.

"Wanna play?" Squeekie hears from his perch.

"Okay!" his own voice answers, and they all race away, deep into the bookstore. Only Midnight remains to guard the way down, her tiny face set in a frown.

The night is long and uncomfortable. It is dirty up in the rafters, full of spiders and dust bunnies, which are not as fun as they sound. It is also uncomfortable in his head, which is full of confusion: why would the Castaways turn on him? Squeekie has always thought he was their hero. They were a bunch of scruffy, orphaned kittens, and he was living a life of comfort and fame they could aspire to. He thought they stayed away because they were intimidated.

Maybe it was just because they didn't like him.

He can also remember a time when things were different. Back when he knew all the names: Mac and Nico, Pumpkin and Beckett, Castle and Creamsicle. They all left in the arms of adopters. He knew he ought to be happy that they'd found homes, but he was a cat, not a saint, and he missed his friends. The obvious fix was to stop making friends. Annika, he now realizes, is trying – but all he has been able to see is an easy way into the snack bin. Oh, stupid Squeekie!

It is in this introspective mood that Squeekie sees dawn pawing at the door. Several hours later, an employee unlocks it and is swarmed by excited kittens. The doppelSqueekie, trailing behind, is eerily unmoved in the face of breakfast, the parceling out of which Squeekie watches with drooling jaws and a rumbling belly. The rest of what he observes that day, between catching spiders in order not to starve, is more disheartening than ever.

DoppelSqueekie:

 1. Is gorgeous. Its coat is the white of crisp, new paper. Squeekie, enshrouded in rafter dust, is invisible to everyone as he lurks above; however, he could wash until his tongue fell off and never look so clean.

 2. Is unfailingly pleasant. At least three kids have tugged on its fur in as many hours. It's hard for a 3-dimensional

cat to match the doppelganger's steady, 2-dimensional charm.
3. Is convenient. Not once has Squeekie seen it move towards the litterbox. Squeekie, stuck in the rafters, has had to do things today that he regrets.
4. Is quiet. Squeekie's famous squeak is absent from the store. Does anyone miss it?

After the lights go out, the paper copy spends the night frolicking with the kittens, seeming to miss neither sleep nor patience as the hours wear on. Midnight has been gone for a while, having quickly lost interest in guard duty. It doesn't matter. By morning, Squeekie has concluded that he doesn't hold a candle to the newcomer. He creeps down the catwalks in the dim morning light, sneezing slightly as the dust is stirred, and into the depths of the James Patterson spillover section where no-one ever goes.

Squeekie puts his head on his paws, closes his eyes, and sighs. At nightfall, perhaps, he will go to the book and take the doppelSqueekie's place. Like the kitten said, it wasn't as though they needed two of him running around.

Something touches him on the elbow as he wallows. "Go away. I give up," he says. He flaps his paw, and it hits something squishy. "Urgh!" His eyes open to see a toad tumble across the floor.

"How rude," the amphibian croaks. It adjusts its waistcoat and goes to sulk next to a stack of books. It is then that Squeekie realizes he is surrounded. A pair of Mary Janes eclipses the view in front of his face; he follows it up to meet the eyes of the telekinetic girl. A pigeon, perched on her shoulder, gleefully munches on a cookie. It gives him a little wave.

Near the end of the aisle, a young man in a robe flicks a wand and whispers, "*Muffliato.*" A quiet seems to wrap around the little group. "There, now they can't hear us."

"Good." The girl crouches down in front of Squeekie and holds out a hand for the cat to sniff. She smells like honey and books. "I'm Matilda, and these guys are The Pigeon, Toad, and Unnamed Wizarding Student #3. Now, are you done with your pity party, or can we get on with solving your clone problem?"

"My – what?" Squeekie's head is swimming.

She sighs. "Look, Squeeks. Nobody's happy with the new management. Plus, I think we can help each other out."

Squeekie shakes his head. He has no idea what is going on, but he does know one thing: "That's not true. Everyone's a lot happier with the new Squeekie. He's perfect!"

All of the book characters exchange glances. "I guess we're just going to have to show you," Matilda says. With Unnamed Wizarding Student #3 ("Just call me Three") leading the way, wand at the ready, they move towards the main body of the store. "*Ascendio*," says the wizard under his breath, whisking the wand in Squeekie and Toad's direction, then at himself. The cat lets out a squawk as they suddenly lift into the air. The muffling spell, however, seems to hold; no alarmed employees or customers come to see what is wrong. They ascend to the level of the catwalks and Squeekie latches on to the nearest wooden plank with his front paws, then wraps his entire body around it. Matilda strolls up on a staircase of levitating books, which then neatly sort themselves back onto the shelves. *Showoff*, thinks Squeekie. The Pigeon, too lazy to fly, rides up on her shoulder.

"Don't move around too much," Three says. "I haven't learned any invisibility charms yet. Plus, I don't think they built these things for people."

"Shhhh. Listen." Matilda puts a finger to her lips.

Voices filter in from up at the counter. A man is fussing at one of the employees. "...at this. I'm bleeding all over the place."

"Sir, those look an awful lot like paper cuts. Are you sure it was Squeekie?"

"I was just petting him, and next thing I know, my hand hurts like the blazes," the man says. Squeekie recognizes him as a regular who is always ready with a scratch under the chin. The volume of his voice is not from anger, but betrayal. "...never done that before..." he hears, before another conversation catches his ear. A pair of Castaways are washing each other's fur beneath one of the bookshelves.

"He's so boring," one complains. The other, mouth full of fur, makes a *mmph* sound of agreement. "And not cuddly at all. If you caught him in the right mood, Squeekie was always up for a good nap. Y'think he ran away?"

Mffffph, the other kitten says.

"Yeah. You got that right."

The Pigeon taps Squeekie on the shoulder. He leans in and whispers, "It's like, you know, someone tried to tell you an oatmeal raisin cookie's as good as a chocolate chip cookie. And you're like, yeah! I like grapes and stuff! And then you try the cookie, and it's SUPER GROSS." Crumbs spray into Squeekie's ear canal. "You're the chocolate chip cookie, by the way."

"Get it? They miss you. I even heard Michelle and Jason say they missed your squeaking," Matilda says into his other ear.

"I guess so." Squeekie frowns, staring down into his beloved bookstore. "Why are you helping me?" he asks. "It's not like I've been very nice to you guys, either."

Matilda twirls the end of her red hair bow. She looks less tough, more like a little kid, as she tries to find the right words. "I've been in a lot of bookstores. We all have. Some of them are big and shiny and perfect, but there isn't a lot of love in them. This place is full of used books, and cats that nobody wanted, and somehow that makes it a lot nicer. You're part of all of that, Squeekie. I don't think it would be the same without you. But," and here she turns fierce again, "if we help you out, you have to promise not to chase us back into the books any more. What do you say, Squeekie the Bookstore Cat? Are you ready to get back on the job?"

They send out Three to set the trap, because he looks the oldest and isn't a small, talking animal. He ambles up and down the aisles as though browsing; it takes a while because people keep stopping him to compliment his "authentic" wizard robe. Eventually, he settles down in a chair and pulls from his robe a book not found on any shelf: *The Next Nine Lives of Squeekie the Bookstore Cat.* The book that released the doppelSqueekie looks brand new in a cover drawn by Matilda, autographed with Squeekie's paw print for authenticity. Now they watch with bated breath as the young man opens the book and begins to read. Squeekie scans the surrounding aisles for his nemesis.

Copy Cat

"Go, go!" he squeaks under his breath, seeing a familiar white shape wander within earshot of the wizard.

Three soon sees the doppelganger as well, and begins to lay out the bait. "I can't believe they'd do that to Annika," he says, apparently to himself. Sure enough, the doppelSqueekie's head turns at the sound of his friend's name. "Squeekie's fans sure are going to be surprised when this one comes out. Wow." He flips a page, sucks in a breath, and drops the book on his lap as though struck dumb by what he has read. "No! Anything but that!"

It is obvious why Three was not the main character of his book, considering his acting skills. Fortunately, it's enough to hook Squeekie's clone. In crafting Three's script, Squeekie tried to plumb the motivations his written self would possibly have. To a book character, what could be more forbidden – or more tempting – than being able to read one's own sequel? And what if they could save their only remaining friend with the gift of foreknowledge?

The doppelSqueekie is visibly agitated now. It draws closer as the wizard stands up, puts the book on the chair, and heads for the bathroom. Unable to handle the suspense any longer, it takes a running leap onto the chair and flips open the pages, needing to see what terrible fate has befallen Annika – and that's when it hears a triumphant yell: "Got you!" Squeekie hurtles down from the shelves above it. Both paws hit the doppelganger in the chest, pushing it back into the book; the covers slam shut, and both book and cat hit the floor together.

"What was that?" he hears from the front of the store. Jason and Michelle come running to see what is the matter. When she sees it is only Squeekie being Squeekie, Michelle sighs, rubs his head, and walks back to attend to their customers.

That evening, after the bell tinkles to signal the locking of the doors, Squeekie sees the Castaways gathered in a dejected huddle on the Yellow Brick Road. They have discovered the doppelganger is gone, and that their machinations have rendered the store completely Squeekie-less. The Siamese clears his throat and is gratified to see all the little ears perk up. He approaches, timidly, and stops in front of Midnight. She attempts to look tough.

"Hi," he says.

She stares at him, expression unchanging.

"My name's Squeekie. What's yours?"

Midnight cocks her head. Then, she smiles. "I knew a Squeekie once," she says. "He was kinda a jerk. You're not like him, are ya?"

"Me? No. Not anymore."

And that, as they say, is that. By day, Squeekie meets with the adoring public, keeps his small friends out of trouble, and naps with Annika, who isn't going anywhere. By night, the bookstore comes alive with a parade of strange creatures and characters. The cats rumpus with Wild Things and debate with Ozma about the merits of their Emerald Kingdom versus hers. The threat of the doppelSqueekie is lost to history.

Except...

When Michelle walks away, Jason does not. Not right away. He lifts the book that has fallen off the chair and takes a good, long look at the cover.

A sequel? he thinks. *Hmmmm...not a bad idea.*

Copy Cat

AUTHOR BIOGRAPHY

Molly Lemke is a student at Wilson College in Chambersburg, PA. She is double-majoring in Animal Studies and Veterinary Medical Technology, and hopes to make a career out of helping people understand and care for their furry, feathered, and scaled friends. Her poetry has previously been included in The Wildwood Journal, HACC's literary magazine, but this is her first published short story. She is also a foster for Castaway Critters, and has successfully adopted out all but one kitten; "foster failure" Ursa also lives at Wilson and is studying for a degree in Studio Art. Her current exhibit, "Claw Marks Everywhere But The Scratching Post," is now on display in South Hall.

Squeekie the Bookstore Cat

3

Squeekie vs. the Stinkie Apocalypse

Jay Smith

This dude at the front door didn't sit right with me.

I mean, I live – *lived* – in a book store where all sorts of folks dropped by. I'm not one to judge because people are people and so long as they don't mess with me or my foster brothers and sisters, I'm happy to see them. I like scritches and treats and the occasional, gentle belly rub and I don't care who's offering.

But this dude: he was not right.

Let me back up.

I live – (sigh) *lived* – in a big cinderblock warehouse. Far as I understood the arrangement, I owned the place. Michelle and Jason ran a book store out of it so they could keep me fed and happy. They did a really good job, too. A lot of people came in all the time to buy books. Sometimes they might scoop a bunch of books into their arms and buy them all. I don't get it, but the books make people happy and selling those books keeps me happy because – food, scratches, toys, and fun.

Well, until lately, that is. But I'll get to that.

Don't give me that. I'm a cat. I'll get to it when I'm ready. *Chill, brah.*

I asked my foster brothers and sisters if their homes are like this and most of them look at me funny. They came from much different places than this or even the streets. When they arrive, they're usually a little nervous or sad but I did my best to share my world with them and get them to relax. I tell them not to mind the grumpy cat – *Annika* – behind the counter but give her a wide berth because, well, she's moody. Most of the fosters call her worse, but I think even Annika has a good heart. She's just...well, a *cat*.

The fosters are cats who stop over here on their way to a forever home. Some of them are a little weird from being alone or abused but I try my best to make them welcome and feel safe. Some are just kittens who don't know anything but the inside of a cage. Others spent their lives on the streets and have a real hard time trusting anybody and, so, spend the most time here waiting for that right person or people to come along.

Right now, my family, aside from Annika, is made up of two kittens, a "chocolate swirl" tabby called *Irving* and his "peanut butter swirl" sister, *Petunia*. They are a bundle of energy and so cute together. We also have *Captain Fabulous*, a mature and laid back Scottish Fold with curly ears and a wrinkled face who was surrendered to a shelter when his hippie owners entered what he called "old people forever camp." Cap Fab is a lot of fun, but likes "the nip" probably a little too much.

Usually, at night, everybody leaves and I get to be alone with my thoughts. I was considering writing an opera or maybe get all of us together to stage a musical version of my first Nine Lives for people. I needed something awesome to follow up my super-awesome bestselling book but I didn't want the same-old same-old.

But one night, Michelle, her family, and a few other folks turned up around the time the moon was high in the sky. They shut off the alarms, but didn't turn on the lights. They looked shocked. I think they were wearing their night clothes. There were three kids, including the boy, and strangers who were a little bit upset about something. I tried to find out what was happening. I went up and began nuzzling Michelle's ankle and asking what the dilly-q, but she was shaking and wide-eyed, like Annika gets in a thunderstorm.

One of the adults, a stranger called Rebecca, herded the kids into the front office while the other adults brought in sleeping bags and cardboard boxes from their vehicle. Jason had a hunting rifle that he held really tight and he kept looking around the parking lot while everyone else moved the boxes into the store.

Squeekie vs. the Stinkie Apocalypse

When they were done, they locked the door and Michelle hung a curtain over it. I protested! How would people see inside? How would I greet them to my home?

But then Jason and Michelle moved a wooden counter in front of the door. I got nervous! What was going on? This was no way to share books with people! While that happened, a horrible scraping insulted my ears and I had to run over to the sunrise side windows by the road where all the vehicles passed to see three strangers throwing books onto the floor and pulling the wooden case away from its spot on the floor.

"Stop it," I squeaked. "Leave those books alone!"

I jumped up on the table where I spent valuable nap time and protested some more. One big man I didn't recognize – he had on a bright shirt covered in flames and motorcycles and had trimmed white face-fur in spots – turned the book case sideways and lifted it. I mean, it was huge! But the man lifted it and brought it toward me. Hands grabbed me and pulled me off the table so the book case could block the windows.

"What's going on," I asked even though I know perfectly well no human speaks Cat.

Except Andrew Lloyd Webber, of course, and he wasn't there to translate.

It was a long night.

Irving and Petunia usually get locked in the pen at night to avoid getting lost in the big, dark bookstore or getting into "mischief" among the bookshelves. That night, though, Michelle let their pen open before joining the other grown up people in the back part of the store, beyond where customers are allowed to go.

Under portable lamps, they spoke in hushed tones about monsters on the streets and how they were going to get out of town and where they could escape because, as Eric said, "This is, like, everywhere."

Leave my home, I thought. *And go where?*

Michelle said no one else was coming because the bridges to Harrisburg were shut down or blocked by...something bad. Jason kept trying to use his cell phone, but he just kept shaking it like it did something wrong. Michelle, who always kept a clear head about things, said, "We have to admit no one else is meeting us here. We have to plan what's next and fast."

I slipped into the small break area up front where three kids whispered to one another about what they thought was happening. A young girl with black hair and glasses – *Shiny*, I think was her name – looked a little shaken up, so I rubbed my head on her leg and told her a joke, which didn't go over well because, as I mentioned, no one speaks cat. The other kids, including Michelle and Jason's kid, were talking about what they saw out on the street. When I walked by to find out what they were saying, they decided it was play time and I kinda lost track of everything with all the pets and the scratches and hugs.

But then Rebecca appeared in the doorway and scared me with a loud SHUSH. The kids were being too loud, she said. I ran out of the room and made my way to the window beside the street.

Tobor was there – did I mention Tobor? No? Well, she was there, sitting at the reading table and peeking out through a gap between the bookcase and the windowpane. Tobor was another rescue foster sibling, though she did her best to pretend not, was a young Russian Blue with a gunmetal gray coat and a secretive nature. She used to tour with a rock band until she escaped the lifestyle and lived on the streets a while.

"Hey, Tobes," I said. "You know what's going on?"

Tobor turned her head toward me, slow, and then fixed me with a blank stare. "The end is coming," she said like someone else would tell me it was a fine night for a walk. She had a thick, posh accent and used big words sometimes.

"The end of what?"

"The end of the world of men," she hissed. "Just like the prophets promised, Squeekie. The souls of the dead will not leave the bodies and so they walk, hunting and feeding on the living."

"Wow." I considered this a moment and then asked Tobor, "That's dark. How do you know all that?"

Tobor turned away from the window and settled down in front of me, wrapping her tail around her paws. She tilted her head to

Squeekie vs. the Stinkie Apocalypse

one side like she was deciding if she should bother explaining.

"It stinks outside," Captain Fabulous said as he hopped up on the table and poked his nose into a small gap in the bookcase. Cap Fab didn't seem bothered by the whole affair except that it stank. He hopped down from the desk to the chair where someone had moved a small bed, and curled up in it.

"The stories of felines passed down from the times of ancient Egypt," Tobor rasped. "The days when the dead would rise and cleanse the Great Kingdoms of people and grant control to the rightful Kings and Queens."

I dared ask, "Who dat?"

Tobor's eyes narrowed. "Why, cats, of course. Not all cats...not you anyway. You're just a servant class housecat. But I will be a goddess to these creatures and rule as I should."

"Whatever, creepy. I'm sure that's an awesome story you tell the other cats on the bus to Metalpalooza or whatnot. Just don't tell that story to the kittens."

Tobor sniffed and hissed and spit. "The rotting flesh of the humans at the dawn of the End Times," Tobor growled at the window. I spotted movement along the railroad tracks across the street. There were a lot of people outside in the moonlight. No cars along the street. No lights at all, I realized. Just the moon and a bunch of people in the dark staggering and stumbling toward the book store.

Someone tapped on the front door of the store.

That brings me back to the dude at the start of my story.

There was a dude at the door. But that dude was not right.

It was the white, milky eyes that bugged me most.

We had this blind foster cat here once with the same look. But this dude kept looking toward the sound of my voice.

"Hey buddy," I said. "We're closed until tomorrow at ten, okay?"

When I paced from one side of the door to the other, he followed me.

"For serious, bro," I continued. "thanks for coming out, but it's a private thing we've got happening in here, okay?"

He reached down to the glass like he might be able to reach

through and, when his fingers bumped against the door, he tried a few more times. I mean, humans can be dumb, but even the dumbest cat won't headbutt a plate glass window more than once. This dude kept slapping the glass to try and grab me.

I hissed and -whoah - he staggered back into a spot where the moonlight shone brighter on his whole body.

Dude was pale and wore the kind of clothes people on the railroad wear when they fix the tracks across the street; one gray jumpsuit that was torn up pretty bad. It was stained around the torn areas with dark red that soaked through the material. It explained why the man looked sick and pale, but it didn't explain the tangle of ivy around his chest and arms or the dead leaves stuck in his hair and clothes. If what he was saying was People language, it was out of words I never heard. He sounded more like a dog out of breath and still pulling against a leash.

"Dude," I said. "I think you need a people vet."

Shadows fell across the doorway and instinct made me jump across the barricade to the opposite side. I heard more of those gargling, hissing sounds that the odd dude made. Suddenly, there were four more sick-looking people at the door, each looking down at me with the same, blank expression and milky, white eyes. They growled like Annika does when she's both hungry AND cranky. They all tried to claw through the glass until one of them got the bright idea to wander off and return with a big rock from the parking lot.

That's when I decided it was time to run away and get a human person.

I was half the way between the entrance and the back-office camping spot area when the banging started. The sound was so loud that it brought the people running. I tried to get their attention as they rushed the door, but they just ran right by me toward the entrance, shouting at each other.

The pounding of rock on glass and metal continued. Every few hits came with the sick sound of cracking glass.

I made my way to the catwalk that runs around the upper part of the building and along the book shelves. A long ramp from the cash register led up to the main walkway that I take when there are too many people for me to deal. I'm not a big fan of the height, but it seemed like a good place to go at the time.

Passing Tobor, I heard her say "When there's no more room in Duat; the dead will walk the Earth."

"*Not. Helping.*" I ran by her and up the ramp. She sneezed and then giggled a bit before returning to her spot on the sunrise window.

The fosters Irving and Petunia were up in the catwalk nearest the ramp staring down in terror. Annika, as usual, lay below us on her bed beside the north side window looking bored. She kept staring out the gap in the wood planks across it and I shouted down,

"How many of those things are out there, Neek?"

She didn't answer at first. She yawned.

"Neek!"

She growled. "Whaaat?!"

"How many people are outside?"

"They is not peoples, stupid. They is... *dead*."

"Sorry, did you say 'dead'?"

"Yaaaaaas," she replied with that tone that suggested I was dumber than she. "Dead peoples walkin' 'round."

"Come on, Neek. You're not down with Tobor's 'End of Days' nonsense, too, are you?"

The kittens squealed. "End of Days?!"

"Dang it," I said under my squeak.

Tobor hissed in the direction of the front entrance. The people were shouting and suddenly the glass shattered.

"Shore up the barricade," Eric yelled. "Don't let them in! Watch their hands, Jason: they've got a GRIP."

A cloud of stink – worse than a spoiled litter box and old cat food combined – passed over us. Ugh, it was awful. It was coming from the front door.

Irving and Petunia huddled together in the shadows, mewing like kittens, puffed up like they were just fished out of a dryer. "What happening," Irving whined. "What do we do?"

"Stay calm," I said. We're up here. They can't get us. Let the people handle it. If it gets really bad..." I paused because I didn't want to think about the really bad.

Petunia insisted, "What, Squeek?"

"There's a secret exit in the basement we can use to get out."

"And go wheres, genius?"

It was Annika. She had jumped out of her bed by the high window and came strutting up the ramp to the landing.

"You can lead the little ones out."

She hissed. "First-o, you ain't the boss o'me. Second-o, what're you gonna do?"

"I'm gonna stay and help the people, our family."

She hissed like a deflating balloon. "What are you gonna do? They was eatin' dead birds and squirrels outside."

A sudden, loud CRUNCH of a wood and metal echoed through the store followed by Eric and Michelle screaming "Get it out of the door! Push it back!" Over their shouts, the sound of moaning grew louder and more desperate.

"Get 'em off me!" Eric sounded scared.

"Hold still!" Michelle yelled over the rising growls and groans. Irving and Petunia huddled up against me, crying as the sound of crushing glass and scraping metal continued followed by a terrible, roar that hit us all with a punch and made everything in the world ring. A wave of pressure pushed me backwards, but I steadied myself. I shook my head to clear the ringing, but it wouldn't go away.

That's when I saw Irving hanging by his claws on the catwalk, a long ways over the concrete floor – like *splat* distance high, terror in his eyes. Petunia was paralyzed with fear. Annika ran for the back half of the store and a better place to hide, her weight shaking the catwalk and making it hard to steady myself.

I turned around and lay on the catwalk, gripping the far side with my front paws and letting my butt and tail hang down over the other side. Hoping that the little guy could hear me, I cried, "Swing up and grab my butt, Irving! Grab my tail and get up here! Petunia help him!"

Irving's rear claws cut into my hide. I didn't want to, but I howled. Kitten claws are like razors but it was a good thing for Irving: the front claws held him to the walkway and the back claws

Squeekie vs. the Stinkie Apocalypse

gave him the leverage to climb back up to the catwalk.

Oh, it hurt. But Irving climbed over me and landed in a ball beside me, purring loud and panting. Petunia sniffed him over and started tonguing his coat at the top of his head.

The ringing had softened a bit and I could hear low, distorted sounds like the dead people moaning through the plate glass – but it was the humans talking. I winced as I turned myself around to see what was happening. My wounds pulled as I bent around but there were Michelle, Eric, and Rebecca around the corner from the entryway. They looked scared and tired... but relieved. With the doorway now a pile of heavy wood and metal, they moved the children back with them behind the curtains in the stock room.

I sniffed the air and scanned the sales floor "Where are Tobor and Captain Fabulous?"

It was at a point where I could hear myself mew, but the ringing persisted. The older cats were nowhere around. No doubt they were hiding and keeping away from the source of the lingering stench in the air.

"You guys stay up here and wait for me," I said. "If you hear me call – you come running. If not, stay until I get you." I didn't want to explain that if the people decided to leave, they'd go fast and I didn't want the kittens to hold everything up by making them search the building. On the other hand, that last break-in looked pretty bad so there might not be time for them to escape. If the stinkies got inside...

I don't know how humans interpret a cat's song. Often, they come running to see what's wrong. Sometimes they throw shoes or yell at us to shut up. Tobor's song silenced the night – even the stinkies outside. They stopped banging on barricades and windows. Tobor's song was equal parts beautiful and horrible. A rough people translation would be:

The power of men forever shed
On the night even Pharaohs dread
When from their graves will come the dead.
The underworld will shut its gate
The dead to hungry bodies, straight

to eat the living they now hate.

There was more, but it got lost in another shattering of glass and splintering of wood.

Before the people could act, the stinkies were inside the book store.

I looked up to the rafters to tell the cats to move to the back of the store – but they were gone. I called out to them, but then the stinkies were past the atrium and in the main aisle.

Tobor was right there to greet them.

She stepped out of the book stacks and sat down about five feet from the first stinkie to appear. It looked like a police officer who rolled down a very big hill and that very big hill was covered in sharp rocks, spikes and razor wire. It focused on Tobor

"Welcome, my children," Tobor sang. "Let us begin the cleansing."

A stinkie in a Batman t-shirt and torn jeans staggered into sight followed by a woman with most of her insides on her outsides. She looked like Annika after a bath, all soggy with hair matted down, pale and milky-eyed like all the others. They looked at Tobor and all three moved toward her.

I didn't say anything as the three knelt and reached for her. I kept an eye on an escape route and any sign of the kittens. Other stinkies were wandering in and surrounding Tobor. She sat there confident and proud, tail wrapped around her paws like that statue she probably imagined would stand for her one day.

The police officer reached out and took Tobor into its grasp, gently and lovingly rising to its feet to turn and share her with the Batman fan and the soggy lady. The short woman in a slick, red cocktail dress joined them in petting and squeezing Tobor. Tobor purred.

But then...

The stinkies hissed. I turned away, hoping that Tobor wasn't so drunk on her weird religion that she didn't see the small gap below her that might let her escape their clawing hands and gnashing jaws.

Whatever happened, I needed to make sure it didn't happen to the rest of us.

Squeekie vs. the Stinkie Apocalypse

Suddenly the people burst out of the stock room with weapons, charging the stinkies with their rifles, a lamp pole, a hat rack, and a baseball bat. All the grown-ups were there except Rebecca who I imagine was watching over the kids.

When the stock room curtain parted, I saw something else that made my heart lighten a bit:

Annika.

That beautiful, grumpy, bitter, old so-and-so. She had the kittens safely off the sales floor and was herding them to the secret escape hatch.

Five of the rotten baddies turned the corner from the entryway into the main aisle joining the first three. The people spread out with their implements of destruction. With new confidence, I parked my fanny at the center of the Yellow Brick Road spiral and greeted them.

"Hello, stinkies! Welcome to my house. Get out before I kick you out."

They reached toward me and began to stoop to snatch me up, intending to tear me apart between them. I fought the instinct to run. They were still pretty far away, but the groaning and the gagging and the gnashing of teeth made it hard to hold my position. I just needed a few more seconds.

"HEY YEAH!" Captain Fabulous peeked out from atop the end cap full of mystery books, hissing and taunting the things. It slowed them down as they tried to work out which of us was the easiest prey.

I caught a scent in the air from behind me. Somehow the first creeps that got inside made their way around the back of the stacks and had me blocked in from behind! Three of the ghouls with only five legs between them staggered out from the kid books and literally fell over themselves trying to get at me. They tumbled to the floor, hands outstretched and clawing at me. I had to bolt for the stacks again but one of the ghouls blocked my way. I had to leap over one's head and dodge a swipe of another's hand, but I made it over them just as the newer group merged with them and they fumbled over one another trying to shoulder their way down the stacks after me.

Cap Fab paced the top of the stacks, howling and humming until two of the ghouls grabbed the end cap and shook it hard. The old cat slipped and tumbled, falling from the top of the stack and disappearing into the crowd with a frightened howl.

I sprinted toward a gap in the books at the bottom of one stack and squeezed through another tight hole between hardback fiction. The left was blocked by two ghouls fighting over stingy remains of something – or someone – but the right way was clear. Unfortunately, it took me back in the direction of the larger mob. I turned to hide back in the stacks just in time to see a gray hand rip through the gap and grab my tail. The grip was so strong, I howled and rolled over onto my back trying to break free. My claws scratched at the concrete as the hand pulled me back toward the shelves. The two stinkies at the end of the aisle saw me and lurched toward me. A pair of dead-eyed stinkies rounded the other end of the aisle.

In any other situation, I would have curled back around and, before the thought crossed my mind, bit into the hand hurting me. But something about that flesh, those bodies, cancelled my instinct. I slashed at the flesh but it didn't respond. I cut deep, but the wounds didn't bleed.

Shadows loomed as the other stinkies closed in around me.

Panic, panic, panic! I dug into the spines of books to keep from getting pulled into the darkness but I fell through and away from the stinkies lunging at me in the aisle. In the dark, I could hear the gnashing of teeth and snarling of the things that probably ate up old Cap Fab. I made confetti out of Raymond Chandler and Raymond Chambers books. The pain made me fight and claw and scrape as I fell backward through the hole...

And then the hand let go.

Terrible crunching sounds, like a folding chair landing in a tub of wet tuna delight. Horrible groans and gurgles. A heavy thud and wet thumps of slip across cement. And the aisle behind me went quiet.

I curled up in a ball inside that dark space. My tail ached and my butt throbbed from where Irving dug into it. I thought about poor Cap Fab falling into that mob. There was no way he could have gotten away, was there?

I didn't even see the guy kneeling, looking into the hole at me. Not a stinkie.

It was the one called Eric – the big man in the shirt covered in fire and motorcycles. "Hey," he said in a hushed voice. "It's okay. We're getting out. Come on."

I wasn't moving. Even as the sounds of crushing and crunching and bashing silenced the growls and snarls on the other side of the stack, I wasn't going anywhere. Too close. Too close to getting snacked on by stinkies.

"Come on, Squeeks," Eric said. "Your family needs you."

That got through to me. Annika, that pain in the butt, was outside with Irving and Petunia. They got out and they'll need me, I thought. Annika was not an outdoor cat.

But I was still scared.

"But what about the stinkies," I whined at Eric.

"Come on," he said. "I'm too big to get in there and get you out."

"That's kinda the point, friend-o."

His round, friendly face stayed in the gap, a small mag light reminding me he was one of the good people.

Someone yelled off to one side. "Are we clear through Science Fiction?"

Another voice called back "I'm all the way in Westerns. We're gold over here. I got Captain Fabulous!"

A warm feeling flushed my shaky bits away at that news.

"Is he okay," I heard Michelle ask.

"Found him trying to claw his way into the catnip box, so...yeah."

Carefully, I creeped from my space in the dark toward Eric and emerged among a pile of silent and limp stinkies. I struggled a bit when Eric grabbed me, but settled down when he put me on his shoulder. "Come with me if you wan'to live," he mumbled and then chuckled to himself. "I always wanted to say that."

All those stinkie people. It was beyond me what happened to them. Eric carried me back to where everyone had been hiding behind walls of hardback books. Eric handed me off to Eric's little kid – Shiny – who noticed the blood on my back and told her mom. Michelle brought a first aid kit over in one hand with Captain Fabulous under her other arm. He looked zonkered on the nip. I wish I had been.

"Dude," Cap Fab said as Michelle put him down next to me on the desk. "Did you see that action, man? It was <u>freaky</u>, man."

"Freaky, sure." I sneezed and started grooming myself to calm my nerves. "Any sign of Tobor?"

"Nope." Cap Fab stretched and rolled onto his back inviting anyone and everyone to enjoy his soft ample belly. Unfortunately for him, I was the one getting all the attention.

Shiny gave awesome pets and her mom and Michelle did their people magic to make the hurt in my butt and tail go away a little before wrapping me in this annoying white ribbon. I know why they did it, but that didn't make me like it.

"What about the other cats," Michelle asked somebody I couldn't see. I wanted to tell her about Annika and the kittens so she didn't worry, but there wasn't much I could do to share. When I felt a little better – had some water and a good tongue bath – I'd head out the secret entrance and try to find them.

"Here they come," Jason called from his spot near the front window.

I didn't know what to make of that and tensed up.

Rapid pops and burps erupted outside and the night lit up with lightning flashes that set my fur on edge. Big rumbling machines and crunching gravel introduced something new outside my house.

"The trucks are coming into the lot," Jason said with a big grin. "Get everybody together!"

Everyone in the place scrambled to gather packs and their bedrolls, gather up boxes with people food and my cat stuff.

Eric's friend Rebecca dropped one of the travel prisons on the desk and said, "Sorry guys. You'll be traveling together for a while."

She opened the small metal gate in the side of the prison and both Cap and I did what we always do when we see it:

Squeekie vs. the Stinkie Apocalypse

Nothing. No way do we travel in those things and certainly not two in one.

Sadly, big hands and quicker reflexes prevailed and we found ourselves stuffed into the prison before we knew it.

But I was too tired to care. Shiny peeped into our prison. She looked as tired as everyone else, but in much brighter spirits. She giggled at how weird we looked stuffed in a box. "It's okay," she said. "We're going to a safe place."

"Do they have nip," Cap asked without a reply.

Traveling by prison is disorienting even when I'm alone. I rarely go outside anymore. Cap and I bumped and rolled against one another as we were carried in a line from the back room to the front of the store. The door was wide open and a bright light made it hard to see what was beyond. We stepped over the stinkie piles and out into the fresh, cool air of the night. The rumbling sound came from big green trucks filling the lot. Some of them had guns at the top and others carried boxes and other people.

An older man in a green and gray uniform, white hair and ice-blue eyes stepped up to our spot in the line, grinning ear to ear at us. He looked at Rebecca, who was holding us, and said, "I'm Major Grant of the United States Army – on behalf of what's left of the United States I am happy to declare you well and truly rescued. And look here! I am such a cat person." He beamed at us. He seemed like such a nice man. He called off to one side. "Sergeant Wake! Put those 'dorbs up in the scout car with me and McInnes. Get 'em fed while we load up."

We said goodbye to the Cupboard Maker Book store one last time. Someone asked if people would ever buy books again. I wondered if I'd ever have such a wonderful home again. We were headed north, I heard one of the soldiers say, to a place with lots of people and even some animals.

We ended up in the back of a long, black SUV. From that per, I watched Michelle and her family load into the back of a truck and Eric's family load into another. Cap kept pressing against my ailing backside and I fought the urge to scratch at him. It wasn't his fault he was big and derpy.

But...I'm just a cat, y'know?

Squeekie vs. the Stinkie Apocalypse

AUTHOR BIOGRAPHY

Jay Smith is an author and award-winning audio dramatist responsible for the Parsec Award-winning horror series **HG World**, the Parsec finalist **The Diary of Jill Woodbine** as well as the pulp adventure serial **Hidden Harbor Mysteries**. Jay's books include the gamer-geek satire **Rise of the Monkey Lord** and the novelization of The Diary of Jill Woodbine. His latest novel is the geek noir thriller **The Resurrection Pact**. Jay holds a Master of Fine Arts from Seton Hill University and is a member of the Horror Writers Association. jaysmithaudio.com

Squeekie the Bookstore Cat

4

Hide and Go Squeek

Eric Hardenbrook

"Hey mister, why are you out here?" The young man strolled up to the ramshackle table set up beside the door.

"Yeah," added the girl walking with him, "Why aren't you in there, where the rest of the books are?"

The man shifted and his folding, portable chair squealed in protest. "I am out here because I get to see all the customers before they even get inside. How much better can you get?"

"Sure, I guess. But it's hot out here in this weather, or humid. I forget," the girl squinted and looked up.

"Yeah, and it looks like it might rain," added the boy.

"Well, I have my portable shelter with me as well," the man gestured up. His shelter looked vaguely like four umbrellas that had been poorly stitched together.

"I guess," the boy didn't sound convinced.

"Well, I'm not here to talk about the weather or shelter arrangements, I'm here to sell my newest book!" the man waved his arm in grandiose fashion across the stack of slender volumes arranged in front of him. "I'm the author of these fine," and just as he was about to launch into his sales pitch the door swung open between him and his potential customers stopping his conversation.

Jay, the other author present for the signing event was holding the handle of the door while chatting with a couple just leaving, "Thanks so much for dropping by folks. Thanks again, I'm sure you'll enjoy all three of my new books. Be sure to stop back and tell Michelle what you think of them." Then he turned and went back into the store pulling the door closed behind him.

"Hey mister, who was that?" the girl asked.

"That was Mr. Smith. He is the other author here for the signing today. Now as I was saying..."

"Yeah, but he's inside," the boy followed on the girl's thoughts.

"Yes. Yes, he is. So is that stupid cat."

"OH! We love the cats!" the girl gushed. She missed the attitude that radiated from the man sitting there.

"Yeah, totally. They're so cool that they climb and get to go wherever they want," the boy looked envious.

"What particular cat do you mean?" The girl asked.

"Squeekie of course. It's the only one that's always here! But I don't want to talk about that, I want you to see the book," and the door opened again to stop the conversation. Smith shaking hands and waving folks off with another copy of his book.

"Squeekie is our favorite!" The boy started again as soon as the door closed.

"Yeah, he's so cute I just want to hug him," the girl hugged herself and twisted back and forth for emphasis.

"He is not cute. He's constantly trying to climb all over me. It doesn't matter when I come in or where I try to set up." The author slumped back into his portable chair. "The very first time I came in for a signing he clawed a hole in my pant leg trying to get in my lap."

"Well, just pick him up. Duh." The boy seemed less than impressed with a single hole in a pair of pants.

"I will not. I don't like cats."

"How do you write books if you don't like cats?" The girl raised a single eyebrow in question. "I thought that was like a requirement or something."

"NO, it most certainly is not." The author leaned forward, warming to this new subject. "Cats and all other manner of pets are a nuisance. They distract from the actual writing."

"No they don't. Ms. Michelle has a whole book of stories about her cat." The boy waved at the poster on the door. "And she keeps a bunch of other ones until they find their forever homes."

"Yes, that's all well and good for her, but I don't like them. I didn't much like the hole in my pants, but I could let that go. The second time I came in I set up in front of the door where Mr. Smith is now. No sooner was the table level then the cat's up there getting in the way and knocking over my soda."

"Oh, you know he didn't mean that, he probably just wanted to help." The girl glanced wistfully at the door. "I really like playing with the cats when I'm here. Sometimes I don't even look at the books," the girl looked ashamed, as if it were some kind of crime.

"That's my point…" and the door swung open between them again. A group of three older children were walking out all holding a copy of Smith's latest book.

"Look, will you two please move a little closer to me over here?"

"Sure, but you wouldn't have this problem if you were inside," the boy didn't seem to notice the glare that comment earned him from the author.

"I was inside for that signing. I couldn't keep anything standing upright on the table. That cat kept knocking everything over. IF he wasn't knocking things over he was yowling and laying down on top of everything."

"Cat's don't yowl, they meow." The girl smiled while she closed her eyes doing her best impression of gloating when one knows the answer and others don't.

"That one yowls. So I moved my table for the next signing. I went to the table back by the bathroom. That wasn't any better - the cat was back there constantly." The author's consternation at reliving the whole scenario was beginning to turn into a sour mood.

"Well, couldn't somebody pick the cat up for you?" They both seemed to think that was an excellent solution.

"Yes, we tried that. The next time I was in I called ahead. I asked them to give me a spot near the shelves holding the staff picks. I thought that would be a much better solution. As it turned out the cat simply leapt down from one of those boards that run all over the place and tried to land on the diagonal shelf. That didn't work entirely as the cat planned so he caromed off that and onto me again."

Both the boy and the girl giggled. "I bet that was funny," the girl added.

"Hardly." The author crossed his arms.

"Well, that still doesn't explain why you're out here," the boy said.

"I tried a table by the door. I tried a table in the back. I tried a table by the shelves up front. No place I went seemed to work." The author leaned forward and put an arm on either side of the table. "So the next time I came into the store I sent a text ahead again. I asked Michelle to let me use a spot in the expansion area toward the back of the store. She was happy to oblige, but no sooner did I set up my little corner back there then that darn cat pokes its head out of the shelf right next to me and tries to climb onto my shoulder! I even brought my own daughter to the store so she could occupy the cat. Squeekie wanted nothing to do with her – wouldn't go near her."

"Wow, he really likes you." the girl sounded so sincere the author couldn't shout his reply at her.

"Yes, but as I stated before I don't like him."

"You should, it would be easier." The boy seemed determined.

"It would not. In fact I took part in another signing day when the tables were all downstairs in the basement and within 5 minutes that cat had tracked me down there and was knocking things off my table!" The author was red faced and sweating. The humid weather was starting to get to him.

"Oh, we don't like the basement it's super creepy," the girl shuddered.

"I like it even if you don't," the boy puffed his chest out. "I went down there during one event and they turned the lights out on us for a whole five minutes" he went on proudly.

"Yes, it's a wonderful and creepy space but still plagued by cats. Now however I have won our little game of hide and seek. I am here and he can't get out to torment me. Listen, I'd like to tell you about the books I've got here," and once again just as the author attempted to describe his work the door swung open.

"There you two are. Would you please come inside?" A kind

looking lady waved her arm at the children, "Come on! We don't have a ton of time today, and besides, it's starting to rain. Let's go!" She smiled and both of the children turned and trotted into the store.

"Good luck mister," the girl waved and pulled her arm back in just as the door swung shut.

The author blew out the breath he didn't realize he'd been holding. How could one miserable cat be such a ridiculous bother? He glanced up as the patter of raindrops began on his shelter. He heaved another deep breath and shifted his table a little further back from the edge of his shelter.

Just as he thought he might be safe and the rain just a passing shower a stiff breeze swept across the parking lot and the rain began in earnest. He glanced up at his shelter while he warily slid some plastic over the top of his books. So long as the wind didn't get out of control he'd be just fine.

As soon as the thought crossed his mind the door swung open and the mother of the two children he'd been chatting with came back out. Her back was to him as she backed up against the door handle and pushed her umbrella out and open. "Come on you two, I told you we didn't have much time," she was waving the two children back out to the parking lot. The boy dodged out to the leading edge of the umbrella immediately sticking one hand out into the rain. The girl was close behind and turned her head to look back into the store. The author stood reaching a hand out toward the door. That's when the author saw the cat. It was Squeekie and he was making a dash for the door.

Just like a movie, the actions of everyone slowed down in the author's mind. The little girl turned and bent to stop the cat from escaping the store. Her mother spun awkwardly in an attempt to both keep her son reasonably dry and out of the rain while reaching back for her daughter. She backed up a half step pushing the door past normal extension. The door knocked into the front leg of the makeshift shelter.

Just as the author shifted and looked up to judge the possible damage the sagging patch in the center of his little roof gave way and dumped the puddle of rainwater directly onto his head. The chilly water made him roar in frustration. He slapped his hands down on the plastic covering his books to save them and turned his now dripping head back toward the door.

In the moment he glanced back he saw the cat stop. Just stop and sit down on the floor. The family bustled out to their car completely oblivious to the author's plight. The author sighed and ran his hands back over the top of his head to push some of the water back up out of his face. At that moment the cat stood up, turned and walked away from the door as if to say, "my work here is done".

"Fine," the author grumbled as he stuffed books back into boxes. "You win this time cat, but I'll be back and next time I'll figure out a place to sign where you won't be able to get at me."

Hide and Go Squeek

AUTHOR BIOGRAPHY

Eric is a fan, an author and an artist, usually in that order. Eric lives in central Pennsylvania with his gorgeous wife and daughter. He writes to try to get the stories out of his head. When he's being a fan he helps run Watch The Skies and assists in the publication of their monthly fanzine. He can be found (at least some of the time) at The Pretend Blog. When not working on those things, Eric enjoys the occasional video or board game and is an old school role player.

5

Everybody Needs a Friend

Carrie Jacobs

Friendship. To Squeekie, it was one of the most important things in the world. He made it his life's mission – all nine of his lives' mission – to befriend all the rescue kitties who came through the book store doors, and help connect them with new human friends. He adored his kitty friends, especially grumpy Annika, and he loved his human friends.

He loved watching human friends come into the bookstore together, pointing out favorite books, helping each other discover new worlds between the pages, and becoming even better friends in the process.

Because he loved friendship so much, his ears perked up when he heard two ladies talking. Squeekie had been napping behind the radio, high above the large-print section, when the ladies sat down at the table, taking a break from browsing.

"Oh, Lois, I don't know what to do. Emma just doesn't seem to be making any friends," one of the women said. Her voice was sad.

Squeekie wanted to jump down and give her a head boop. Those always made the humans feel better. But he stayed where he was and listened.

The woman continued. "She's always got her nose in a book."

The second woman chuckled. "She got that from you, you know."

"It skipped a generation. My daughter hardly reads at all. I'm glad Emma likes to read, but she needs some real friends."

"It must be hard on her, moving in with her grandma while

her parents travel the world. Especially in the middle of the school year," the second woman said kindly.

"It is. It's worse since her brother is a social butterfly. He had new friends the first day."

"She'll find her place, Sue. Just be patient."

Squeekie had never met Emma, but he felt bad for her. He peeked over the wall, hoping to catch a glimpse of the ladies. His eyes widened with recognition. They were both regular customers. He got up and stretched, then took the short way to the front counter. He had an idea.

Squeekie was on a mission. He landed on the counter with a soft "thud" and nudged a stack of papers until it fell over, spreading the pages across the counter.

Annika poked her head out of the basket she had been napping in. "What are you doing?"

"Looking for someth- here it is!" He placed his paw on the paper and pulled it free from the scattered stack.

The ladies arrived and placed their stacks of books on the well-loved wooden counter. Sue patted Squeekie's head. He tapped the paper with his paw. "Here! Give this to Emma," he said.

Annika snickered.

Sue kept petting him, but didn't look at the paper.

"Look. At. This." Squeekie spoke slowly, carefully enunciating his words.

"Ooh yes, you's such a good kitty, isn't you?"

Annika rocked the basket with her laughter. "You know they don't understand you, Squeekie. You give people way, way too much credit."

"Help me, Annika, this is important!"

With an inconvenienced sigh, Annika gracefully jumped out of the basket and stretched. She tiptoed over to the counter. "What are we doing?"

"She needs to see this." He tapped the paper.

Annika cocked her head. "I'll try." She hunched her shoulders and started making an awful horfing noise.

"What are you doing?!"

Horf! Horf! Horf!

Everybody Needs a Friend

The hairball landed in the exact middle of the page. Annika grinned at her handiwork. "You're welcome."

Squeekie stared at the blob in horror. "Oh no, you've ruined it!"

"Poor kitty," Lois said, reaching out to pet Annika, who narrowed her eyes in warning. The woman paid no attention, and was rewarded with a small scratch to the back of her hand.

Annika jumped to the floor. "Well, I tried."

Squeekie sighed. "Thanks, I think."

"Eew." Michelle threw the paper in the trash and scratched Squeekie's head. He looked around, trying to find something else that might work. There was nothing.

The women paid for their books and put them in their canvas store bags. Squeekie watched Michelle drop two nickels into the can beside the register. "Since you brought your own bags, the rescue gets a nickel for each of you."

Sue smiled. "Here's another dollar for the can. It's such a good cause."

"I have something important to tell you," Squeekie yelled at Sue.

"Oh yes, you're such a talkative little fellow, aren't you? I'll bring some treats for you and your friends next week."

"Bring Emma with you," he pleaded.

She scratched his chin and baby-talked to him. "You's such a good boy. Such a sweet widdle boy. Yesh you is."

Exasperated, Squeekie turned and walked across the counter, stepped onto the cash register, then jumped up onto one of the cat perches and made his way to the top of the shelves, where Annika was hiding.

"I don't know why they insist on talking to me like that. I'm highly educated. For Pete's sake, I live in a *bookstore*."

Annika's eyes widened in surprise. "You sound upset. That's not like you."

Squeekie tucked his paws under his belly and settled himself down, wrapping his tail around his side. "I feel bad for Emma. She doesn't have any friends. Everybody needs friends. Even you."

Annika thrust her back leg out and licked it. "I suppose you're right. What's the plan?"

Squeekie shook his head. "I'm going to sleep on it."

"Good idea. I'll join you." She curled up and purred them both to sleep.

Squeekie had just gotten comfortable in his hiding spot, away from a rambunctious new tuxedo kitten, when a familiar voice made him perk up.

He listened closely. It had to be Sue.

"This is the bookstore I was telling you about, Emma."

"Wow, Grandma, this is awesome."

"Go look around. Try to stay under budget."

Squeekie peeked around the corner, trying to catch a glimpse of Emma. He trotted toward the YA section at the back of the store. He scurried around the corner, coming face to face with a well-worn pair of pink Converse sneakers. He looked up into a pretty face framed with long brown hair. Her bright blue eyes crinkled at the edges, behind black framed glasses, as she smiled at him. She hunkered down. "Hi, kitty."

Squeekie gave her his best purr and wound around her legs, wrapping his tail around her ankle.

Emma scratched Squeekie's head. "You're such a pretty kitty. So friendly."

"What about me?" The new kitten bounced over, jumping and spinning, his tiny tail straight up in the air, his eyes wide and excited. He pounced at the fingers Emma was wiggling at him. "What about me? Am I pretty? I think you're pretty. You have a lot of strings. I love strings."

Squeekie chuckled. "Simmer down, Sammy, humans can't understand us when we talk."

"How come? Why not? That's silly. We can understand them, so how come they can't understand us? Huh, Squeekie? How come?" Sammy was attacking Emma's shoelaces while he talked a mile a minute.

"Sammy, let's go so Emma can look for some books."

"Aww, do we hafta?"

Squeekie nodded.

Everybody Needs a Friend

"Fiiiiine," Sammy gave Emma's shoelace one last swat and darted away.

Emma laughed as she watched him go. Satisfied, Squeekie rubbed against her leg and walked away. He stayed close, though, peeking at her through the aisles, listening to her hum. He liked her voice. She seemed happy, browsing the aisles, reading the backs of books and making a stack on the front counter, but Squeekie knew her grandmother was right. Emma needed some friends.

Ones that lived outside the pages of a book.

Emma picked up a book and flipped through the pages. She added it to her pile. Squeekie watched her stand and wrestle with the stack of books. She carried them to the front of the store, where her grandmother was chatting with Michelle.

Squeekie jumped up on the counter and rubbed against Emma's stack of books. He purred while she scratched his head.

"Have you read the Study series by Maria V. Snyder?" Michelle was asking Emma.

"No, what are they about?"

Squeekie sat down while Michelle raved about the series. "Maria's amazing. And she's going to be here for a book signing next weekend."

Michelle slid a flyer across the counter and Squeekie pounced on it, meowing loudly. He took another step to a pile of flyers and stepped on the one he wanted. "Give her this, too!" He kneaded the paper, crinkling the corner.

"Good idea, Squeekie, you're so smart." Michelle scratched his chin and handed an un-kneaded paper to Emma. "We also have a Teen Book Club, if you're interested."

Squeekie head booped Emma's hand and gave a loud meow.

Emma laughed. "Looks like Squeekie wants me to sign up."

He purred and rubbed his cheek on her hand.

Sue patted her granddaughter's shoulder. "That sounds wonderful."

"Here's the current book they're reading." Michelle handed her a copy to look at.

Emma smiled. "I've actually been wanting to read that." She

added the book to her pile, along with a copy of Poison Study.

"We should get going, we have to pick your brother up." Sue paid for their books and put them in her canvas store bag while Michelle dropped a nickel into the can.

Emma nodded and folded both flyers and stuck them in the pocket of her jeans. "Maybe I'll see you next week," she said to Squeekie.

"I hope so," he said, knowing she only heard him meow.

Squeekie watched her push the glass door open and leave the store. He curled up on the counter.

"Was that your genius plan?" Annika poked her head over the basket.

"Yep."

Annika gave him an approving nod. "Not bad."

The next weekend, Squeekie scampered to and fro, showing off his new bow tie, carrying out his host duties for Maria's book signing. The door opened a hundred times, customers and fans filling the store and lining up to have their books autographed.

Squeekie shook his head at Annika, who was perched on the windowsill in the foyer, wanting everyone to fuss over how pretty she was, but not touch her. Annika nodded her head toward the door. "Here she comes."

The door opened and Emma and her grandmother walked in. Squeekie ran over and rubbed against Emma's leg. She petted him, then followed her grandmother to the counter, where they purchased the rest of the books in the Study series.

Emma got in line to have her books autographed.

Squeekie grinned when he saw another girl about her age get in line right behind her. "Come on, come on, start a conversation."

"Have you read any of them?" The blonde girl asked Emma.

"Yessss!" Squeekie did a little bounce.

Emma turned. "Me?"

"You're Emma, right?"

"Yeah. Yes. I just read the first one. I'm sorry, I just moved here and I'm not sure what your name is."

"Cassidy. We have chem together. Where'd you move from?"

"Colorado. I'm living with my grandmother."

"Me, too." Cassidy laughed. "*My* grandmother, not yours. So you liked Poison Study?"

"Ohmigosh, I couldn't put it down. I can't wait to read the rest of the series."

Squeekie watched the girls for a few minutes, then went to mingle with the crowd. When he came back, they were giggling and talking like they'd known each other for years.

"You should come to the book club," Cassidy was saying.

"I might. I started the book you guys are reading, but I haven't finished it yet."

"Once you hit the middle, you won't be able to put it down. You'll definitely have it done before the next meeting. Let me get your number." Cassidy pulled out her cell phone.

Emma pulled hers out, too, and they exchanged numbers.

"I'll add you to my Goodreads, too."

"Awesome," Emma answered.

Squeekie was rather pleased with his success. He straightened his bowtie and went off to enjoy the rest of the party, hoping someone would drop a piece of cake so he could clean up their icing. He kept an eye on Emma and Cassidy. They chatted until they reached Maria's table and got their books signed.

Squeekie had to laugh. When Emma reached Maria, she got tongue-tied and star-struck. Cassidy nudged her arm and whispered, "She's super nice. Relax."

He watched as they left the signing table and stuck together, both of them talking incessantly.

A few days later, Squeekie and Annika sat side by side on top of one of the bookshelves, watching the nine teenagers laugh and talk and discuss books. Emma exchanged numbers with everyone in the group.

"Did you hear the good news?" Squeekie asked. "Sammy got his forever home. Emma's grandma adopted him. He's going home with them tonight after book club."

"That's wonderful," Annika said, swishing her fluffy tail. Sammy was under the table, attacking Emma's shoestrings. "She really seems to fit in."

Squeekie nodded. "I'm so glad."

"Me, too. I know what it's like to be uprooted from the only home you've ever known and get dropped in a strange place. It's not easy."

Squeekie settled onto his belly, remembering how frightened Annika was when she'd arrived at the bookstore. He watched the kids clean up their books and paper and smiled as Emma scooped Sammy up and kissed his head.

Sammy wriggled and caught the string of her hoodie in his mouth. He caught Squeekie's eyes and grinned. "Bye, Squeekie! Bye, Annika! I'm going home with Emma!" he mewed.

Squeekie waved good-bye to him. "Your story has a happy ending, too, Annika."

"Only thanks to you. If you ever tell anyone I said this, I'll deny it. But you're right. Everyone needs a good friend. Even me." She yawned. "I'm glad you're my best friend."

Squeekie started to answer, but Annika was already pretending to be asleep. He leaned over and gave her a light head boop. "Me, too."

Everybody Needs a Friend

AUTHOR BIOGRAPHY

Carrie Jacobs began her writing career at age three, when, still lacking the dexterity to form recognizable letters, she dictated a riveting tale to her transcriptionist, AKA Mom. "A Frog Named Tog" rocketed to #1 in the family, but did not garner international acclaim. It did, however, serve as an early clue that writing would be a lifelong journey.

Since then, she spent approximately fifteen years as a columnist for a local weekly newspaper, writing "slice of life" type articles. She also frequently write articles for a local non-profit. Carrie has won two first-place awards through Pennwriters.

She loves writing contemporary romance novels, and writes short stories in any genre imaginable, including the weird and creepy. Her settings are many places she's visited and her hometown, all thrown into a blender and poured out into the place she would most love to live. Her characters are people she knows, would like to know, or would like to avoid.

Carrie lives in beautiful central Pennsylvania with her family and spoiled pets.

Connect with her on Facebook at facebook.com/writercarriejacobs, on Twitter at @carrieinpa or on her website at carrieajacobs.com.

6

Squeekie and the Mermaid

Lynne Reeder

The day I met the mermaid began like any other. Books yawned as they readied themselves for sleeping all day while sunlight peeked over the windowsills. Dust particles danced in the still air as the front door opened, keys jingling in Mother's hand as she called out to us. I stretched. Annika rolled over, puffs of unruly gray hair covering her eyes. I shook my head and gave her a gentle pat as I moseyed out to greet the humans. Another morning at Cupboard Maker Books was under way.

Hours later, the front of the store exploded with people. A long table held an entire row of bustling, breathing, busy "authors," as Mother kept calling them, and their chatter circled above my head much like it did at night, when there were no people and the books awoke and spouted their stories to the still night air. I readied myself for a boring day of interrupted napping, because I could tell this was an "event" as Mother always called them, and lots of the adult humans would be taking up space today.

As I circled around my bed atop the large wooden table in the far corner, she entered. The cinderblocks of the walls immediately tingled, and my fur stood on end. Not in fright, mind you. More like in anticipation. You see, cats sense magic. It's why I drift on the sea of books' voices every night and know that this little girl holding that tall woman's hand is not an ordinary human.

The girl twisted her foot and tugged on her mother's bag. I inched closer, hoping she would pull the bag free and deposit it on the floor because I love to snoop through bags. People have all kinds of amazing things with them. My movement caught her eye and she glanced my way, and a ripple flowed through her blue irises. It cascaded over me and I closed my eyes for a moment, soaking it in. Just like when someone pets me just right. I opened my eyes and stared at the little girl. Her smile burst across her face, and I turned to head back to the large wooden table, knowing she would follow me.

I jumped into my bed and circled, tucking my tail beneath me. Her face swam into vision, close enough that her eyelashes almost tickled my nose. "Hi, kitty," she said. Her hand landed upon my head, and I pushed into it so she'd know it was okay to pet me. "You're so pretty. I love your bowtie."

I smiled at her, then meowed. This was the true test. An ordinary human would hear my voice as a simple meow. But someone with magic would hear it cascade, like a slow dripping out of their ears. I watched from beneath her hand as her eyebrows furrowed and she turned her head to the side. She shook herself, as if she hoped to dislodge the last trickling drops of my sounds. I smiled wider. I had been right. This little girl was magic.

I placed my paw on her extended forearm and her attention shifted back to me. Once again, her irises rippled, the ocean contained in her reacting to her movements.

"My mom told me your name is Squeekie." She studied me closely.

I nodded.

"Can you understand me, Squeekie?" she asked. Her hand still rested lightly on my head. My paw slipped from her skin.

I nodded.

"Does everyone know that you can understand them?"

I shook my head.

She beamed, and while I'm sure the adult humans noticed nothing, the lights flickered brighter at that moment. Her hair shimmered and her hand released the space between my ears as she ran back toward the front of the store. As her feet traveled the concrete stretch, they blurred ever so slightly. When her foot was extended down, a shape took form in that split second: not legs, but a severed tail. I gasped.

Squeekie and the Mermaid

This girl was indeed full of magic. She was one of the last mermaids.

She came back to me before I could fully process this realization, markers and paper spilling from against her chest. "Squeekie, I want to be an artist when I grow up," she gushed, throwing her supplies onto the table. She reached over to me and adjusted my blue bowtie. I sat up a little straighter. "And I want to draw you, if you don't mind because you're beautiful. Do you mind? I mean, can I draw your picture?"

I nodded, and she shimmered again, a faint glow emanating from her pores, much like the way the books glistened at night once everyone left and they knew it was safe to begin their whispers. She glided into the chair and picked up a black marker. Its scent drifted between us as she drew my outline. I meowed again to ask how the magic felt as it sang in her blood.

"What, Squeekie? Are you hungry? I'll go ask my mom for my snack." Hm. She didn't seem to be able to decode my meow. For the first time in a long while, frustration tied my tongue that I didn't speak the same language as the humans. With magic, she should be able to transform my meows into human words. And she most certainly had magic because there was that blurriness of movement again, that faint memory of a tail radiating around her stride, so why wasn't she--

Unless she didn't *know* she had magic. I buried my nose against my chest and threw my paw over my eyes. Of course. She had no idea the power she possessed. She was only a young girl. She wouldn't be able to control it even if she *had* somehow figured it out. The books in the store only spoke once they reached ten years after their publication date. The younger ones watched enviously as the older ones fluttered pages and spewed their stories through the air. The books kept up front, the brand new ones not even a year old, simply laid there without a trace of consciousness. This young girl must have just begun developing signs and hadn't yet learned to recognize them. I knew I needed to make her aware; what greater gift could someone give to a little girl than her own magic?

She returned, trailing salty breezes in her wake. She held her closed hand out to me, and I peered more closely, sniffing. Beneath the beachy air clinging around her shoulders I could make out my favorite of all scents: treats. Mother must have heard her and given her a few to entice me with.

"I'm Maya, by the way," the little girl said, placing the treats on the table in a straight line. I plucked one into my mouth, taking one step forward to reach for the next. I walked along, munching the treats as she talked. "I always wanted a kitty but I think my dog would not be so nice so we can't get one at our house. Is this your house? Do you live in the store? My mom would love if a bookstore was her house. Books are her favorite." Maya placed the last treat just above the edge of her drawing paper. I snatched it up, then sat facing her. My tail switched back and forth. "Me, I love art. Do you like my picture so far?"

I nodded.

"Thanks!" She picked up the black marker again and went back to work. My ears took shape, along with my bow tie, my eyes, my whiskers. I loved being her subject. I switched my tail some more.

My tail! That's how I could tell Maya she had mermaid in her blood. I jumped down and rubbed against her legs. I circled around both instead of weaving in between like I normally do to people, because I wanted to send the message of her legs *together*.

She giggled. "Squeekie! Come back up here, I'm not done with your picture."

I meowed, my thin voice surging like a wave toward her. Her brows furrowed. "Are you trying to tell me something, Squeekie?"

I nodded and meowed again, circling her legs, pulling them tight as a net would. I stared into her eyes, searching for the ocean I knew was there, begging her to make the connection. I wished she would be here at night, when the books awoke, because I knew they would tell her what I couldn't.

"Maya!"

The woman she had entered with walked toward us. She had her bag on her shoulder, keys jangling in her hand. "Hey, girl, it's time to go. Whatcha got there?"

"I drew a picture of Squeekie." Maya turned back to her

portrait, scribbling with her blue crayon across the outline of my bowtie. "Do you like it?"

"Um, I don't like it." Her mom picked it up and examined it from various angles. She looked at Maya, grinning. "Because I *love* it. C'mon, let's go show Michelle. She's going to love it too."

Maya jumped up and grabbed her mother's hand. My tail slipped from around her ankles, my chance ebbing away. I followed her back to the front of the store, listened to Mother gush over the portrait, saw the glory on Maya's face as Mother hung the portrait of me front and center behind the counter. Maya's joy glittered around her.

I searched the shelves as Mother talked about writing and placed books on the counter in front of Maya's mom. There! On the bottom shelf, a row of children's books. I meowed until Maya noticed me. I rubbed against the book spines. They'd lecture me about getting my fur in their glue but I didn't care. Time was running out.

"What is it, Squeekie?" Her hand landed on the top of my head. I leaned into her for a moment, and she sunk to her knees, crouching so that we were face to face.

I rubbed the books again.

"You want me to look at these?"

I nodded. She scanned the titles, tipping them out to see the covers. "Oh, Squeekie!" she exclaimed, pulling out a copy of *Beauty and the Beast.* "How'd you know this is my favorite?" Another book tipped over into the empty space left from the volume now clutched in her hands. The end of Ariel's tail peeked out from the shadows. I meowed furiously and batted at it.

Maya picked it up. "*The Little Mermaid?*" I nodded and rubbed against her elbow. You, Maya! You! You're a little mermaid!

Her eyes glinted. "I'm gonna ask my mom if I can get these!" And off she ran.

Did she know? Had I done enough? I sat by the bookshelf, trying to decipher that glint. She handed her mom the books then ran back to me.

"Thanks, Squeekie," she whispered, "for letting me draw you." She glanced back at her mom, who was paying for books she'd grabbed as Mother had been hanging the picture. "And thanks for telling me."

I shook my head, decluttering the words she'd just spoken. Did she say--? But I thought--?

"I didn't want anyone to hear us. But I heard you." She smiled. "And don't worry. I've always known what I am." She reached beneath the neck of her purple shirt and pulled out a shell necklace. As she unfurled her palm, the shell glowed. I met her eyes, and the tides in her irises swelled with the secret we now shared.

Her mother came up to her then, holding out her hand, and Maya kissed me on the head, tingles traveling down my spine before she skipped out the door, adventures calling at her heels.

Squeekie and the Mermaid

Squeekie the Cat by Maya Reeder

Lynne Reeder

AUTHOR BIOGRAPHY

Lynne Reeder experiences the world with a writer's heart and an artist's eye and never goes a day without composing a poem. She earned her MA in Creative Writing from Wilkes University. Poet Laureate of her hometown for 2016, her works have appeared in Mothers Always Write online magazine and Her Heart Poetry literary journal, as well as in the Strange Magic anthology published by Sunbury Press. Poems of hers are among those published in Paragon Journal's [Insert Yourself Here] anthology, The Soapbox Volume II, and Genre Urban Arts inaugural publication. Lynne resides in central Pennsylvania with her high school sweetheart husband, their two energetic daughters, and their quirky pitbull. She spends her days valiantly trying to pass along her lifelong passion for reading and writing to her secondary English and creative writing students, where every now and then great life truths make themselves known--which is what literature is really about, in the end. *Found Between the Lines*, Lynne's collection of short stories, essays, and poems, all paired with pieces of her blackout poetry, is currently available online. You can find more about Lynne and her works at www.lynnereeder.com.

7

Squeekie in Mageia

Kiera Lehman, 8th Grade

Squeekie crept toward the door and peered in at Lisa. Lisa was sitting on her bed, reading what looked like the last page of a book. Squeekie had noticed that Lisa hadn't gotten a new book lately, so they were bound to go back to Cupboard Maker Books and get a new one. Lisa loved taking Squeekie there so he could talk with Annika and the other cats.

Lisa had adopted him from Cupboard Maker Books last year. Lisa regularly visited Cupboard Maker Books and all of the humans there knew her. They also knew Squeekie, and Squeekie knew the other cats. Annika was the store's adopted cat, so she would always live at Cupboard Maker Books. The other cats were foster cats, so they came and went. Squeekie missed Annika and his other cat friends, they were company, even if they almost always left the store to go to a new home. He turned his attention back to Lisa as she snapped her book shut with a loud sigh.

"Dad, can I take Squeekie over to Cupboard Maker Books?" Lisa shouted to Ted, her father. He was a small man with grey hair and a huge smile. Ted never said no to Lisa's trips to Cupboard Maker Books. He walked in and picked up Squeekie.

"Okay, Lisa. But you have to promise that you'll come back right after. It's getting dark, you know. And you have to do the dishes when you come back," Ted added quickly. Lisa nodded and took Squeekie from Ted's arms. Squeekie yawned and squirmed in her arms to get comfortable. Lisa retrieved her money and, with Squeekie in her arms, started toward Cupboard Maker Books.

When they finally got there, Squeekie jumped to the ground and stalked over to Annika.

"Annika. How's the store? Any new books?" Squeekie asked, sitting down next to her. Annika opened her eyes and laughed.

"Squeekie, you're back! I've missed you. New books, huh? Well, we do have a new fantasy book. I heard it's a good one," Annika said thoughtfully. Squeekie thought for a moment.

"Okay, I'll see if it's worth reading," Squeekie decided finally. He found the book and looked around to make sure that no humans were around to see him. When he saw none, he pawed gently at the book and it fell to the ground. Squeekie jumped down and pawed to the first page.

Once, there was a world full of magic. This world was called Mageia. Mageia will always exist, but it may be forever forgotten. Mageia contains all sorts of magical creatures, from sphinxes to pixies, from dragons to humans. Humans are very, very rare in Mageia. Once, humans from Earth were allowed to travel to Mageia, but they became violent and they feared the magical creatures, so they tried to kill them or capture them as pets. They routinely traveled to Mageia and were enchanted with the beauty of the lands. In fact, the Ancient Greek word 'magic' was only named that way because of Mageia. But the humans were destructive and violent. Now, humans cannot travel between the worlds. Earthly creatures, however, such as dogs or lions, birds or cats may still travel to Mageia due to their peaceful and innocent natures.

Squeekie shook his head at the nonsense written down on the page of the book sitting at his paws. Of course there was no such thing as a world of *magic*. He pawed to the next page out of curiosity and sneezed, because of the golden dust that rose from the pages. A tinkling sound started to come from the book. Squeekie hissed and tried to close it, but he couldn't move. A golden light poured out of the book and then-

Squeekie opened his eyes and tilted his head. Where was he? He stood up and stared at the forest surrounding him. He was in

Squeekie in Mageia

Mageia! Squeekie growled in frustration and pawed at the ground. He didn't want to be in Mageia, he wanted to be at Cupboard Maker Books! Lisa would be leaving soon, and if she couldn't find him, she would be absolutely devastated.

"Hello there, little cat!" Squeekie jumped at the sweet voice that had just chirped in his ear. He looked up and immediately spotted a small glowing creature hovering close to him. It resembled a human girl, but it had very large pupils and its skin was tinged pink.

"How can I get back to Earth, please?" Squeekie asked politely, not wanting to anger the petite creature. Appearances can be deceiving, and he had a feeling that this creature could be a threat. He assumed that it was a pixie, based on the passage of the book that he had read. The pixie laughed before tilting her head up toward the sky and whistling.

"Why would you want to leave Mageia, silly cat? Mageia is the *best* place in the *universe*! My name is Piper, and I've called my friends, and we're going to take you home so we can have fun together, and you won't *want* to leave!" Piper exclaimed happily. Squeekie felt the hair on his back rising.

"No, Piper, I *do* want to leave!" Squeekie protested, eyes growing wide as he spotted the mass of pixies nearing them. Piper shook her head in disbelief. The pixies now surrounded her and Squeekie could hear her loud, enthusiastic voice urging the pixies to 'take him home'. Deep blue dust settled on his fur and he felt his eyelids grow heavy. The last thing he felt was a strange floating sensation.

"Oh, he'll want to dance with us, won't he, Merry?" Piper's voice woke Squeekie from his deep sleep. He jumped up and looked around him. He was in what appeared to be the sky, and he was laying on a cloud. There were thin walls surrounding him, but no roof or floor, and there were small flowers everywhere, floating in the air and decorating the walls. Piper squealed in excitement as she noticed that Squeekie was awake. She was floating beside a pixie with green skin and cream colored hair. He wrinkled his nose and inspected Squeekie.

"I don't know, Piper. He doesn't look like much fun. I don't know why everyone's so excited about this cat," he said after a moment. Squeekie shot a glare his way and sat down on the cloud. He hissed as he fell right through and floated underneath the cloud, which was already reforming. Piper laughed and ducked under the cloud to join him.

"Oh, I'll bet you're *really* fun! Don't mind Merry. He doesn't realize how *special* it is to have a *real* Earth-creature here in Mageia!" Piper said breathlessly. Squeekie sighed in frustration.

"I just want to go home, Piper. It was a mistake coming here. I was just reading that book, not trying to actually come here," He explained in what he sincerely hoped was a patient voice. Piper frowned and flew behind him to pull on his tail. Squeekie hissed and jumped, causing him to float up into the cloud. Spluttering, he somehow managed to propel himself upward a safe distance away from the bothersome cloud. Just then, three more pixies entered the 'room'.

"Ooh, Piper, is this the Earth cat that we brought here? I didn't get a good look at him on the journey, you know," a pixie with light blue hair said, staring at Squeekie along with the others. The tallest flew above him and sat on his head, smoothing down Squeekie's hair.

"It's so cute! We should keep it," it said loudly. Squeekie shook himself, causing the pixie to fall off of him and bump into the smallest one. The tall pixie glared at Squeekie. Two more pixies joined them.

"Oh, what's the commotion, Piper? This cat looks very grumpy," one of the new pixies observed. Squeekie turned to Piper, a plan in mind.

"Well, Piper, my friends say that I'm pretty boring, actually, and I don't know why! Sure, I take naps most of the day, but other than that, I love to quote useless facts!" Squeekie lied, fighting back a grin. Piper looked horrified.

"Well, you *do* like to dance and sing, don't you? You'll *love* dancing and singing with us, right?" Piper asked nervously. Squeekie laughed in response.

"Are you making a joke? I *hate* singing and I abhore dancing! Oh, if I had to sing, I would just scream!" Squeekie continued, still holding back his grin. Piper, however, was clearly not amused.

"Oh, I've had enough of *you*. Tiki, Merry, and Flutter, take him down to the ground. He can't stay with us anymore!" She shouted before flying away at top speed. Three pixies stayed behind, but the rest followed Piper. The pixies each sprinkled pink dust on him and when he blinked, he was startled to discover that he was on the ground. The pixies were nowhere to be seen, but he realized that he was definitely *not* where he was supposed to be.

"Oh, hush, Sil. He's just a cat, like us! He looks lost. We need to help him," a quiet voice disrupted the silence. Squeekie's ears perked and he tilted his head. A cat stepped into the clearing that Squeekie was in and smiled.

"Hello, my name is Jingle, and this is Silver, but we call her Sil. Are you lost?" Jingle asked, looking concerned. Squeekie slumped his shoulders in relief.

"Yes, I am. I'm from Earth, you see, and I came here through a magical book. Pixies kidnapped me and took me with them and I've just now escaped. I don't know where I am, though, and need to get back to the portal as fast as I possibly can," Squeekie explained. Jingle and Silver shook their heads sympathetically.

"Oh, those pixies. They're always causing some sort of trouble! It's that Piper. She's their little ringleader," Silver hissed. Squeekie nodded in agreement. Jingle and Silver sat down to think.

"You'll want to head east. When you reach the river, follow the stones north. It's that simple. You'll probably run into the dragons, so if you find yourself near one of their nesting grounds, do *not* wake them, whatever you do. I hope you find the portal. Good luck, Squeekie," Jingle added before jerking her head toward Sil. They both disappeared back into the forest. *Go east until the river, then follow the stones north. I can do that,* Squeekie thought to himself. With a worried look toward the forest where Jingle and Sil had gone into the forest, Squeekie headed east, the opposite direction.

Squeekie was making good time. He could detect a river, about a mile ahead of him, but he also sensed something that smelled an awful lot like smoke, and it was close. Dragons, for sure. They were the only danger that the cats had warned him about, and they would have mentioned any other form of fire.

"Oh, just sleep, Ash. It's time to go to bed. I don't want another word out of you!" a deep voice growled. Squeekie froze.

"But, Mama-" a second voice complained, but the first cut it off.

"Or I'll tell your Pa to ground you from using your fire for *one week*," the first voice said. The voices stopped and Squeekie moved forward slowly and quietly. They were obviously the dragons. Squeekie would have to be very, very quiet and careful. He crept forward, inch by inch, freezing once he spotted them. Giant creatures with long snouts and deep red, scaly skin. These were surely dragons. Squeekie silently crawled through the grass. A sharp intake of breath made him freeze. His eyes darted to the smaller dragon, who was watching him with wide eyes. Squeekie and the dragon had a 'miniature staring contest' as Lisa would call it. Finally, the small dragon grinned and closed its eyes. Squeekie smiled to himself as he ran as quickly as he dared, putting as much space between himself and the dragons as he could before stopping to take a breath. He collapsed in front of a tree and closed his eyes for a moment, but he didn't have much peace.

"Well, well, well. What do we have here? A little kitty, isn't it? Wake up, little kitty," A sly voice called softly from behind him. Squeekie's eyes flew open and he turned around to face the creature. A goblin! Squeekie was certain that it was a goblin. It had bumpy, green skin and long ears. Its long, knobbly fingers reached out to stroke Squeekie's ear.

"What soft fur, little cat! Does the little cat want a rat? Who's a good kitty? Yes, you are," the goblin goaded Squeekie on, grinning in amusement. Squeekie flashed his claws to the goblin and offered a frown.

The goblin cackled and jumped from foot to foot, looking strangely delighted. Once he stopped hopping, he put his hands on his hips and frowned.

"Kart'Muk doesn't like grumpy cats! Bad cat. I'm going to take you home, yes, and you'll be my pet! You'll be my pet, and you'll never leave!" Kart'Muk giggled. Squeekie turned away and tried to continue his journey to the river. Oh, he could smell it! He could

Squeekie in Mageia

hear the rushing water! He was very close.

"No, no, no! You're coming with Kart'Muk!" Kart'Muk shouted, grabbing Squeekie's tail. Squeekie growled and swiped his claws toward Kart'Muk in anger. Kart'Muk dodged the claw.

"Okay, kitty. I'll let you go if you can solve this riddle. A murderer is condemned to death. He has to choose between three rooms: the first is full of raging fires, the second contains assassins with fully sharpened spears, and the third has many lions who haven't eaten in ten years. Which room is the safest?" Kart'Muk asked gleefully. Squeekie thought for barely a moment before the answer came to him.

"Obviously the third. If the lions haven't eaten in ten years, they're dead by now!" Squeekie said happily. Kart'Muk shouted and stomped his foot. A crack appeared in the ground and, with an angry huff, he jumped down. Alarmed, Squeekie peered over the edge. He saw a small bed and a fireplace before the hole closed up. Chuckling to himself, Squeekie continued on his way to the river. He soon arrived and followed the stones north. The stones were perfectly round and had glowing symbols in the middle of each of them. He followed the stones into a forest. He knew that he was very close to the portal. He soon found the clearing with the swirling blue portal, and he was soothed by the sight of it. Squeekie ran to the portal and dived in headfirst. Squeekie was going home.

"Squeekie, wake up!" Annika shouted in his ear. Squeekie opened his eyes and shouted in relief. "Annika, I'm back! How long was I gone? Has Lisa been worried?" Squeekie asked nervously. Annika frowned in confusion.

"Squeekie, you must've been dreaming. Was the book really that boring that you fell asleep? You haven't left the room, and you and Lisa only arrived about five minutes ago!" Annika said, standing up and jerking her head toward Lisa, who was running a finger along the spines of several books in the fantasy section. "Oh, no, Annika. I went to Mageia! I met pixies, fairies, and a goblin! I've been gone for *hours*. Days, even. Maybe there's a time difference?" Squeekie asked, suddenly unsure. Had it all been a dream? Had he dreamt the whole thing?

"Squeekie, time to go!" Lisa shouted, gently putting some books into her homemade bag and turning toward Squeekie. She must've paid already. Squeekie said goodbye to Annika, but he was distracted. He thought during the whole journey home before coming to the reluctant decision that it had all been a dream.

"Oh, Squeekie, what's gotten on your fur? Is that glitter?" Lisa asked as she carried him inside. Squeekie leapt from her arms to the ground and ran to the floor-length mirror in her room. Surely enough, his fur was shimmering with blue, pink, and gold glitter. Squeekie knew then without a doubt that Mageia was real.

Squeekie in Mageia

AUTHOR BIOGRAPHY

Kiera Lehman is a budding author living in Enola. She enjoys reading fiction books and writing stories. She reads about 200 fiction and fantasy books per year. Her favorite genre to write is fantasy. Kiera lives with her parents and two dogs. Kiera wants to someday become a teacher and writer. Kiera is a freshman at East Pennsboro High School and has many friends there. Her favorite class is, of course, English class.

Squeekie the Bookstore Cat

8

Squeekie and Abbey

Stella Phillips, 7th Grade

Squeeks woke up from his morning nap with a start. He yawned, not feeling fully rested. Squeekie was about to have another nap when he heard a high voice squeal his name. A small boy, maybe 6, was peeking at him from beneath his bed. Squeeks sat up and smiled at the child. The boy petted Squeeks gently, grinning from ear to ear. After the child had left, Squeeks prepared for a nap.

Finally, Squeeks thought, *I can enjoy a well-deserved nap!*

Yawning, Squeeks stretched in his cat bed. Suddenly, he heard a small voice whisper to him, "Squeekie! Wanna play?!"

Squeeks lazily rolled in his bed to face Claire, the small tortoiseshell cat with a playful attitude.

"I suppose," Squeeks said. *Why can't I just have a nap?!* He thought.

Sluggishly, Squeeks hopped off his blue cat bed and stood next to Claire. She grinned at Squeeks devilishly and tackled him. Squeeks and Claire play fought in the middle of the bookstore. Bella ran over, her black tail flying behind her.

"Squeekie! I need your help!" Bella cried. Squeeks and Claire stopped fighting to face Bella.

"Why can't I help?" Claire demanded before Squeeks could reply.

"Claire, you're just a kitten! You don't know anything!" Bella said.

Claire stared at Bella in shock. "I do too know things!" Claire cried, "I know that you think you're better than us!" Bella and Claire began to fight, and Squeeks stood in between them, trying to break up the fight.

"Ladies, come on," Squeeks said, "Let's all go. Bella, show us what you need help with."

Bella led them to the back of the bookstore. They turned left and reached the area by the bathroom. The trio crawled under the table with several chairs surrounding it. The owner human was setting up for the meeting the humans had with books. She laughed at the group of cats playing under the table.

"I found something under here," Bella said, her eyes big and serious.

"What is it?" Squeeks asked, feeling impatient and tired.

"I don't know," Bella said, "I've never seen anything like it before!"

She pawed at one of the floorboards. A piece pried off, revealing something small and silver.

"There's words on it," Claire said, pawing at the key.

Squeeks leaned close to read it. "Secret room key," Squeeks read.

Claire stared at him blankly. "What does that mean?" She asked.

"I'm not sure..." Squeeks answered honestly, "Do you know what it means, Bella?"

Bella shook her head. "No idea."

They stared at each other, unsure of what to do. "We can't leave it here," Squeeks finally said, "The humans are having a meeting here. They'll catch onto us."

"I have the perfect spot for it!" Claire said, picking up the key with her mouth. Squeeks and Bella followed Claire as she hurried to the other side of the store. They went behind the curtains hung up in the back. Claire jumped on top of a pile of books and dropped the key into a box.

"Are you sure no one will find it?" Squeeks asked.

"I doubt it. With the meeting, they'll probably be distracted," Claire said.

They waited until after closing time, when everyone had left

Squeekie and Abbey

the store. The three hurried to the key's hiding place. Bella picked it up and dropped it onto the floor.

"What do you think it does?" Claire said, staring at the key.

"I think it has magical powers," Squeeks theorized, "Maybe it will give us endless cat treats!"

They stared at the key with hope. The key didn't do anything, so the cats moved on from staring.

"Hey," Bella said, "Why don't we use that large screen the humans use to find out stuff?"

"You mean the square thing?" Claire asked.

Bella nodded, and they plodded to the counter. The screen was black, so Squeeks moved the "mouse" as the humans called it. The screen lit up and asked for a password.

"Do you guys know the password?" Squeeks asked.

The cats stared at each other, confused. Claire jumped onto the keyboard to get a better look at the screen. She stomped on many keys at once, and the screen made a loading sign pop up.

"What happened?" Bella asked, peering at the screen from the countertop.

"I think ... we started it up," Squeeks said, putting his paw on the mouse. He moved the arrow around, trying out the new contraption.

"I've seen the humans do this a million times," Squeeks said, pulling up Google, "You just type in what you want to find out, and this screen pulls up answers!"

Bella and Claire gazed at the computer in awe as Squeeks tapped the keyboard. He typed "key" into the search bar and read the definition that first appeared. The cats scanned the definition.

"It's used in a lock ..." Bella said when she finished.

"A lock? What's that?" Claire asked.

"I guess we should look it up," Squeeks said, turning back to the computer. He typed "lock" in this time.

Again, the cats read through the definitions.

"I've seen this before! Follow me!" Claire cried.

The cats ran away from the computer and followed Claire to the back of the store. They climbed to the top of the bookshelves to a spot hidden by a cat bed. Claire pushed the cat bed off the edge and pawed at a small square door with a lock on it. Bella, holding the key in her mouth, jammed it in the lock. It took several tries for them to figure out the correct way to fit the key in. Slowly, the door creaked open to reveal darkness on the other side. Nervously, Squeeks entered first, in case something dangerous lie ahead.

A small voice rang out from the darkness. "Hello? Who's there?" Said the voice.

"M-My name is Squeeks," said Squeeks, filled with bravery, "What is this place?"

A small light flickered, and Squeeks could make out a grey cat holding a candle.

"This is the heart of the bookstore," she said, "My name is Abbey, and I watch over this lovely place."

Bella and Claire entered, looking scared.

"Squeeks? Is it safe?" Claire whispered.

"Of course!" The grey cat exclaimed.

"This is ... the heart of the bookstore," Squeeks explained, "Her name is Abbey, and I guess you could call her ... the watcher of the bookstore."

Abbey smiled warmly. "That's a good way of saying it. I stay here, making sure everyone finds the right book, and occasionally, cat."

She snapped her fingers, making the room light up dimly. "I was once a stray here, waiting to be adopted," she said, "But then I discovered this room ... and the powers that came with it."

"Powers?" Squeeks asked, confused.

Abbey grinned and made a cat treat appear in front of Squeeks.

"I have powers," she said, "I can make people happy, place protection spells ... you name it!"

Bella swiped the cat treat up and ate it. Squeeks glared at her, and Bella simply said, "I was making sure it wasn't poisoned!"

Abbey laughed and led them to couches just the right size for a cat. They each sat on one, still nervous about the stranger with mystical powers.

After a long silence, Abbey finally spoke. "You know, there's a reason you are here," she said, her tone suddenly serious.

Squeekie and Abbey

"What's that?" Claire asked, stretching on the couch.

"I can't control this power by myself ... it's a lot of responsibility, and I often find that I make little mistakes. I need help with my job," Abbey explained, "Which is why ... I wanted to ask Squeeks if he would take some of my power, and help me to watch over the bookstore, to help preserve its charm and magic."

Bella and Claire looked over at Squeeks, who was shocked at the request. "You want me to be the guardian of the bookstore?" He asked.

"Yes," Abbey replied, her face lit up, "You're like the store's mascot. It seems appropriate to appoint you as the keeper of the store's magic, too. So, will you be my partner in the protection of the bookstore?"

Squeeks smiled and answered, "Of course. This place is my home, my happy place. I care about it so much!"

Abbey took Squeek's hand and led him to the center of the room. There was a pedestal that seemed to glow with power, and on the pedestal was a collar. The collar was light blue with red, white, and navy blue stars. Abbey revealed her own collar, which was a sparkling purple with silver flecks.

"These collars symbolize power and protection. Wear this and you can access your magical abilities. Just make sure to be careful when using your power. It's strictly forbidden from human eyes," Abbey explained, putting the collar around Squeekie's neck.

"Why can't the humans see it?" Squeeks asked.

"Humans abuse power," Abbey explained, "They don't know how to love without hate, or how to rule without greed. It's a flaw that barricades them from magic."

We went silent as we heard a creak.

"Opening time," Claire mumbled, getting up from her couch.

"Already? How is that possible?" Squeeks asked, peeking out the secret door.

"This room was made so that time passes by quicker than normally. You must go! I can't be discovered! Farewell, my friends, and always remember that I'm watching over you!" Abbey said, shutting the door and making it blend in with the wall. A small child spotted the three cats on top of the book shelf.

"Hi kitties!" he cried, pointing. Squeeks jumped from the bookshelf to curl around the child's legs. The boy giggled and rubbed Squeekie's back. Squeeks' collar glowed as the boy petted his back.

A book fell from the shelf and on to the floor in front of them. The child picked it up and hugged the book to his chest. He ran to show the book to his parents, and the cats watched him go.

"Was that you?" Claire asked.

"I ... think so," Squeeks replied, gazing at his collar.

They heard someone whisper a "Psst!" and looked up to see who it was. Abbey was peeking out from the doorway. She winked at the trio and disappeared back into her secret room. The cats smiled and went their separate ways, looking for more people to meet and offer affection.

Squeekie and Abbey

AUTHOR BIOGRAPHY

Stella Phillips is an aspiring young writer who often spends her free time lying in bed reading a good book or writing her own. When she's not writing or reading, Stella enjoys drawing, spending time with her family, and listening to 60's and 70's classic rock. In addition to this contest, Stella has placed second in post level in the VFW Patriot's Pen contest.

Squeekie the Bookstore Cat

9

The Battle of the Bookstore

Hannah Chapman, Sophomore

The door of Cupboard Maker Books closed and was locked with a click. Squeekie, who had been asleep in his cat bed by the window near the "Reference Books" section, bolted awake. The time to act was now. The gray Siamese cat with piercing blue eyes got up out of his cat bed (of course he stretched, like all cats do), and jumped down from the table to find his friend Annika, a fluffy cat with an attitude.

"Annika," Squeekie called. "It is time. We must hunt the enemy now."

There was no response. Squeekie roamed the aisles of the store, quickly trotting along to find his fluffy friend.

"Squeekie! Let us come with you! Please!!!!!!"

Squeekie, confused at first, followed the sound of the tiny, desperate voices. It didn't take long to find out what the source of the noises were. He stopped at the end of the Sci-Fi/Fantasy section and looked up to his left. There he saw the two little kittens up for adoption, Pepe and Poppy.

Not these rascals again, he thought. When they first came into the store, Squeekie told himself he would try to be tolerant of the new arrivals. He was normally tolerant of all humans and other cats, but for some reason, these two got on his nerves occasionally.

"Listen. There are a few reasons why you can't come along. First of all, you are very young, and have little to no experience of-" Squeekie paused. Should he reveal what the mission was? "...of roaming the store at night," he finished weakly. He knew it was no good as soon as he completed his sentence.

"We know that's not what you're up to tonight," said Pepe defiantly.

"Yeah, there's more to just 'roaming the store at night'," said his sister, Poppy.

"Maybe there is. It's no business of yours. You two aren't Permanents. You're just Temporaries." Squeekie said. The "Permanents" currently consisted of both him and Annika; they were the permanent bookstore cats, and were not up for adoption. The "Temporaries" was the term that Squeekie and Annika used for the cats that would soon be leaving the store to find a new home. It was somewhat of an insult to remind other cats that they were Temporaries. While the cats up for adoption would eventually get a nice home, it seemed that the Permanents were a tier above any cats up for adoption in the bookstore.

With that last word to the kittens, Squeekie strutted off in search of Annika.

At the moment, Annika was fast asleep in her favorite place: on top of a cart, surrounded by mysteries and various nonfiction books. Squeekie went past the shelves with Employee Recommendations, past Trade Paperbacks, past Annika, and into the back room. Just when he was wandering behind the curtain, Squeekie heard the door of the store open.

Who could that be? He thought. *The store just closed fifteen minutes ago.*

All Squeekie knew was that he had to act normal: go up to whomever walked in and meow at them until they pet him (and then meow some more).

Little did Squeekie know that Annika had woken up and was listening intently for any hint as to who walked in. As Squeekie walked past Trade Paperbacks, Annika jumped down from her spot and rushed over to him.

"Squeekie!" Annika stage-whispered (yes, she stage-whispered). "Wait for me!"

Squeekie paused and waited. Annika quietly stayed behind

The Battle of the Bookstore

Squeekie; she would be back-up just in case whoever walked in was harmful. They snuck quietly up the Yellow Brick Road to the front of the store. Just paw steps away from the Hogwarts emblem on the floor, they heard a sound that Squeekie had not heard for a few years; a metal sword against the leather of a sheath.

Squeekie turned around, and Annika looked at him with confusion written across her squashed face.

"Go now," Squeekie said quietly to her. "Go up the catwalk. Stay quiet. I'll explain what I can in a little while when the coast is clear."

"But Squeekie – "

"Just do what I say! Now is not the time to argue."

Squeekie ran off to the back room, angry and disappointed with himself. Why hadn't he told Annika about the history of the bookstore? Battles had been fought of which Annika should have been informed long ago, when she first arrived at the bookstore. It was too late now. Another was beginning, and there was no time to waste.

Squeekie's tiny brain was buzzing with thoughts. For weeks after the last battle, Squeekie had formulated a plan and recited it to himself every day so it would be imprinted in his mind. However, he eventually stopped going over it.

Why? Why do I do these things? I should have told Annika about this, and I should have memorized the plan better! Squeekie thought to himself.

Now was not the time to blame himself. He rushed into the back room, and ducked behind the curtains that marked the boundaries for customers. He paced back and forth, trying to organize a plan.

There's no way Annika and I can fight alone. That's the first problem. I need reinforcements, he thought.

Then, Squeekie remembered. He recalled what he had done so long ago on that awful night. He ran even farther into the back to a hidden exit in the wall leading to the outside. As he stepped into the warm summer air, he momentarily forgot what he had come out to do; at that moment, he saw a bird. Squeekie began to chase after it, then remembered that the bookstore was in danger. He needed to call for help. Squeekie performed his signature meow (a long, wailing note), and was soon met by his old companions. The first to appear was a rather bony, but tough, orange cat named Scruffy.

"It's happening again, isn't it? An attack?" he asked Squeekie.

"Yes. This time, though, I am not prepared. I forgot my plan; do you remember anything that worked last time?" Squeekie asked.

Scruffy was not the one who responded, however. Another cat had made his way towards Squeekie, a tuxedo cat named Pippin.

"Running around on top of shelves and knocking books over worked just fine, I think," Pippin answered confidently.

His sister Alice, a calico with gold specks throughout the black fur on her back, walked up to his side and gave her thoughts as well (it's important to keep in mind that she is a cat who gets scared easily).

"Some should stay back and be look-outs. You know, not get too close to all the action," Alice suggested timidly.

Pippin looked at her with amusement clear on his face. Alice ignored him. They were brother and sister, but did not treat each other well. Pippin always chased her around, barely giving her a chance to fight back against him, enjoying how easily it is to scare her. Hopefully this wouldn't interfere tonight with serious matters at hand.

Squeekie directed their attention to himself once again.

"Thank you all for these suggestions and thank you for showing up. This bookstore would not be standing if not for all of you. It is time to defend it once more against the enemy, and show them that we are not afraid. No matter how many scratches we endure, we will keep fighting! Just think: if we can endure hairballs and full litterboxes, we can take scratches."

The speech seemed to invigorate the surrounding cats. They all pawed the ground restlessly, ready for action. Squeekie began to give them orders.

"We will enter through the secret entrance I just came through. Scruffy, I want you to take two cats with you and climb on

The Battle of the Bookstore

top of the 'Romance Paperbacks' shelf. Sneak to the end and keep an eye out from up high. Hiss if there is danger; then, follow my lead and attack. We don't know how many of the enemy there are; I only heard one enter, and I'm sure he was the leader. There will definitely be an army."

"Yes sir!" Scruffy said, grinning. He was ready for the fight; this is what he lived for. As a stray cat, he spent most of his days going after other animals and getting into tussles. Squeekie returned the smile, and continued instructions.

"Alice and Pippin, I want you to take the remaining two cats and walk quietly into the main area. Follow the Yellow Brick Road and make your way to the catwalk. You'll find Annika somewhere on the catwalk; she'll join you. I'm going to sit on the counter, watching for the enemy – that is, if he hasn't already advanced past the store entrance, which I'm sure he has."

Alice looked scared, but Pippin was ready, his eyes filled with fiery determination to finally do something good. Pippin wasn't exactly a well-behaved cat at home; his owners had gone through a lot of trouble with him.

"We're ready, Squeekie. It is our duty as cats to unite against the enemy," Pippin declared.

"I will do the best I can, Squeekie. As my brother said, us cats stick together no matter what," Alice said, still timid, but with a stronger voice.

"Excellent. Time is running away from us though. We must hurry; Annika has no clue what's going on. I should have informed her about our history. But this is no time for regret now! Now is the time that we fight!" Squeekie said resolutely.

The cats entered through Squeekie's secret door and took their positions. Scruffy and his partners climbed stealthily up to the top of their shelf. Alice, Pippin, and their fellow cats gathered up their courage and slunk to the ramp to climb onto the catwalk. Squeekie followed behind them but continued to the counter where he sat waiting for the first glimpse of the enemy. He sniffed the air, but there was no scent of anything suspicious.

Where is he? He thought nervously. Just as this thought flitted across his mind, he heard a low hiss coming from nearby. It was coming from the catwalk. Tom, one of the cats accompanying Alice and Pippin, was staring intently towards the Western section; his fur was on end. This was it; the time to act was now.

"Pippin, if you hear me, jump across shelves until you reach the Western one," Squeekie stage-whispered.

Squeekie sat still, poised for action. Then he saw it; a long pink tail flew out of sight around the corner of the Western section. Squeekie hopped down from the counter and followed it. He had a bad feeling about doing this, and he was right. As he turned the corner where he saw the tail disappear (near the table that he had been taking a leisurely nap on earlier), he realized, too late, that it was a trap.

Five rats, each about a foot and a half tall (these were no normal rats), were standing on their hind legs holding swords. They were wearing tiny battle helmets, as well as wooden shields on their sword-free arms. Squeekie felt a rush of fear; the enemy was much more prepared than last time. He turned to run, but three of the rats rushed forward and lifted him up by his tail. Squeekie flailed around, and knew he needed back-up.

"Pippin! Alice!" Squeekie yelled.

"We're coming, Squeekie!" Pippin responded.

Pippin began knocking over the hardback adventure books at random, hoping they would meet their marks. Two of the books hit two rats squarely on their heads, knocking their battle helmets off. Stunned, they let go of Squeekie's tail. The last rat let go; Squeekie was simply too heavy for him. Squeekie ran for it. He made it behind the counter and up onto the catwalk. He called for the others to regroup, and he met them near the entrance to the store. Distantly, he could hear Poppy and Pepe whimpering in their cage; the rats were bigger than they were.

"We know how many are here now," Squeekie said. "The leader has brought five rats with him, but I don't know where he is. He was the one I heard walk in the door. Right now, we should follow Pippin's lead; knock the books over. Their helmets are strong, but can still be knocked off. Then we can scratch and bite them until they become scared enough to run away. There's no way we can kill them. I want each of you to run in different directions on the catwalk and go to random sections of books, preferably hardback sections; those books will do the most damage."

The cats nodded and obeyed. They could spot a few of the rats taunting Pepe and Poppy. As much as Squeekie was bothered by them, he ran off towards the Hardback Mysteries and shoved as many books as he could at the rats down below. They were caught off-guard; by the time they turned around, the books were flying at their faces. Squeekie kept pushing books off the shelf until he was sure they wouldn't be able to get up with the weight of them. He would deal with this group of rats later.

Meanwhile, Alice and Pippin had spotted two rats in the Sci-Fi/Fantasy section. They (and their fellow cats) quickly began heaving books into the aisle below.

"Why aren't you fighting back? Come on rats, you can do better than this!" Pippin taunted, grinning, as he thrust a heavy book (*Fellowship of the Ring* by J.R.R. Tolkien) towards the floor. As soon as he said it, he felt a sharp jolt of pain in his back leg. He collapsed on top of the shelf, feeling something snap as he did so.

"Pippin!" cried Alice. She ran over to him, knocking over books carelessly (one of which was a well-known book by Lewis Carroll).

The snap that Pippin had felt had come from an arrow (about the length of a pencil with a sharp thumbtack attached to the end) shot by the fifth rat. While it was only a thumbtack, the arrow had been shot with immense strength and struck Pippin hard.

Squeekie had heard the commotion. He rushed over to Pippin and Alice and told the other cats to keep fighting. The two rats that Pippin had been fighting were in the same situation as the first two rats. There were still two rats left; the one who had shot Pippin, and the leader. Squeekie looked at Pippin, feeling guilty (by calling the other cats here, he felt it was his responsibility if they should get hurt) but determined to help him. He told Pippin to stay put; the rest of the cats were going to keep fighting, and would tend to Pippin after the battle ended.

Hopefully we are the victorious side, Squeekie thought to himself miserably. He was proud of how well the cats had fought so far. The battle would be over soon.

Squeekie motioned for the cats to regroup again. He told two of them to go off looking for the last small rat, and instructed the rest of the group, including Alice and Scruffy (Annika was still hiding somewhere on the catwalk), to join him to find the leader. The latter group crept into the back room, keeping their eyes and ears open for any sign of the big rat. That's when they heard it; a slithering sound in the very back corner. Squeekie knew at once what it was; the leader's tail. Squeekie motioned for them to follow him; Alice, full of anger from her brother being harmed, walked bravely right beside Squeekie, and Scruffy was right behind her, followed by a few other cats.

As they walked down the Romance aisle, they heard the sound that Squeekie had heard earlier: the sound of a metal sword being drawn from a leather sheath.

Did the rat really double back to come up behind us? Squeekie thought.

His thoughts were soon confirmed. The cats turned slowly together to see a large rat, about two feet tall, with a steel helmet and sword, as well as a wood and metal shield. His teeth gleamed in the little light there was in the back room, and his eyes glittered menacingly. It was the leader.

"We have been hated on by cats since the beginning of time," the rat said in a raspy voice. "Now, we fight back. We fight for the smaller ones of our species."

"We will fight back!" Alice yelled back. "One of yours hurt my brother, and you're going to pay!"

"You're never coming back to our bookstore!" Scruffy shouted up at the rat.

With these words, the cats jumped at the humongous rat. They scratched, bit, and clawed what they could. Alice had jumped onto his shoulder and tipped his helmet off with her paw, and Scruffy hung onto the shield. Squeekie struck the rat across his face while the other cats clawed his back. The rat fell over from the force of all the cats that jumped on him. They stood on top of his chest and glared down at the now defeated face of the rat.

"This is our bookstore," Squeekie told the rat. "Cats are the symbol of this bookstore, not rats. Stay away, unless you want a repeat of tonight."

The Battle of the Bookstore

The rat began to back up, and the cats got off of his body. He stood up, and ran as fast as he could with a heavy limp to the front door. The cats followed him, and met up with the two cats that had fought the small rat.

"Did you get him?" Alice asked.

"Yes," said one of the cats. "He ran out the door a few minutes ago, along with the other four. We lifted the books off their bodies and warned them to never return."

"Thank you," said Squeekie. "It is important that we hold true to what we think is right. We will not kill the rats; however, we will warn them to stop coming here. They will eventually learn that we are stronger than them, and their attempts to defeat us are futile."

A moan of pain was heard after these words. It came from Pippin; he had tried to stand up on top of the shelves in the Sci-Fi/Fantasy section.

"Quick!" Alice said. "We need to get him down."

With the combined efforts of all of the cats, Pippin was half carried, half dragged down the catwalk. Squeekie took a look at his leg.

"The arrow definitely snapped when he fell over," Squeekie said worriedly. "We need to remove the rest of it. Luckily the end is still poking out. We can pull it out with our teeth. Scruffy, can you help?"

Scruffy had the pointiest teeth, so he would be the best cat for the job. While the rest of the cats held Pippin down, Scruffy bit down firmly on the arrow and pulled with all his might. The arrow came out, and the wound began to bleed. Squeekie ran to the bathroom and came back with a paper towel.

"We'll have to try and bind his leg the best that we can so he can get home," Squeekie told them all. "The owners will take care of him from there, right, Alice?"

Alice had been sitting silently watching them take care of Pippin. She was terrified.

"Y-yes, they should," she said shakily. "They're wonderful people."

Squeekie nodded, and directed the cats to tie the paper towel around his leg. Pippin stood up unsteadily, but found he was able to walk. Alice breathed a sigh of relief, and looked at Squeekie.

"Thank you, Squeekie," Alice said. "I don't know what we would have done."

"It is I who has to thank you," Squeekie said. "All of you, thank you for your courage. I hope that this will not have to happen again for a while, or even ever again. The rats must learn their lesson, and we must keep teaching it."

"Hear, hear!" came a tiny voice from the distance.

Poppy and Pepe were watching everything from their cage.

"I have a question, Squeekie," Pepe said. "You said you would be 'roaming the store at night.' What were you hiding from us?"

"Oh, that? We were going to go chase some mice." Squeekie told him, smiling. "I just wanted to make it sound like something much better. Sadly, we were interrupted by rats."

The cats all looked at each other and laughed. They were relieved that the fight was over, and eager to get back home. One by one, they walked off into the back room to exit through the secret gap in the wall. The cats exchanged goodbyes, and Squeekie watched them walk off into the distance. When he turned around, he saw Annika standing behind him.

"You have a lot to explain," said Annika said, smiling. "There is a lot more to this bookstore than meets the eye."

"You aren't wrong about that, Annika," Squeekie replied. "I should give history lessons. What do you say we include Pepe and Poppy? They may be Temporaries, but they're young. They should love tales like these."

"So when do we start?" Annika asked eagerly.

Squeekie woke up the next morning, sore but refreshed. The sun was shining through his favorite window, and the sky was bright blue and cloudless. It was impossible to think that last night, a battle took place that would go down in the history of the bookstore (at least, in the cats' minds). Squeekie lay there, wondering how the cats were doing. Hopefully Pippin and Alice made it back home alright.

The sound of a door shook Squeekie out of his daydreams.

The Battle of the Bookstore

"What happened here?!" exclaimed a voice.

Oh no, Squeekie thought. *The books on the floor. This should be interesting.*

But nothing further was said. The owner of the bookstore, Michelle Haring, had carried on with her normal routine of setting up the bookstore for the day, and the books were shelved without comment.

The door opened again. The familiar "Hello, let us know if we can help you find anything" rang through the air; this was Squeekie's signal to begin his day job. He stretched (hesitantly; his whole body ached from the fight), and ambled over to the customer who walked in. It was time to live up to his name and squeak at the customers, something you would not expect from a cat that had led his fellow felines into battle the night before.

Hannah Chapman

AUTHOR BIOGRAPHY

Hannah Chapman has been an employee at Cupboard Maker Books for a little over two summers. She currently goes to Mary Baldwin University and plans to major in some kind of biological field, and maybe one day do research for NASA. Hannah loves any kind of pet, especially cats (two of her cats, Pippin and Alice, are in her story in this book). She loves to read, with some of her favorite books being the *Harry Potter* series, "Hidden Figures," and the *Ranger's Apprentice* series. Hannah also loves any kind of outdoor activity, from soccer to tennis, or hiking to swimming. Her favorite cat at the bookstore during the time she has been there was George, a black and white kitten who is a lot like her cat, Pippin (named after the hobbit. Hannah enjoyed playing fetch with him while working and watching him chase after other cats. Hannah is ready to start working at the bookstore again when she comes back from school on break, and is ready to see what new cats are at the bookstore then.

10

Squeekie: Cat Detective

Lindsay Grubb, 12th Grade

It was a frigid winter night in Enola, Pennsylvania. The clock had just struck eight o'clock and the Cupboard Maker Bookstore was closing. Squeekie was curled up in his normal corner, trying to keep warm as the workers locked up the store and trudged out into the cold parking lot. Once the door slammed shut, Squeekie padded around the store to make sure that the coast was clear. It was! He then began the hunt for his nightly read.

"How about a mystery novel?" Squeekie thought.

The shivering cat dashed over to the Mystery section and began to look for a book. After searching through a few books, such as *The Westing Game* by Ellen Raskin and *The DaVinci Code* by Dan Brown, he eventually decided on *Nancy Drew: The Clue of the Velvet Mask* by Carolyn Keene. Quickly, he lugged the book back to his toasty corner and began to read.

"*You look lovely, Nancy, and very mysterious,*" *said Hannah Gruen, housekeeper for the Drew family, as she smiled fondly at the slender, titan-haired girl. Nancy had just finished dres-*"

'THUD!'

A loud noise echoed from the front of the bookstore! Squeekie was terrified but intrigued at the same time. What in the world could be happening in the store at this hour? As he ventured towards the commotion, he tried to disregard the phrase, "curiosity killed the cat."

Peering around the corner of a bookshelf, Squeekie was able to see a man, dressed in black from head to toe, slamming his shoulder into the front door of the store. After trying this a few times and failing, he went to extremes. He used his right hand to break the glass on the door and unlock the shop from the outside! Scared out of his mind now, Squeekie hopped up on top of the bookshelf so he was out of sight, but could still see what was happening down below.

The tall, skinny man crept into the shop and looked around. Before doing anything, he surveyed the store just to make sure that no one was inside. Good thing that Squeekie was hiding! After making his rounds, the ominous figure shuffled to the front desk. He dug through the papers and books on the surface, but ultimately took interest in the large, silver cash register. The robber drew black leather gloves from his pocket and put them on his hands. Then, he broke into the register using only his hands! Quickly, he snatched whatever was in the register, threw it in his bag, and raced out of the store.

Squeekie was devastated! He knew that the owners of the bookstore worked so hard every day to earn that money. They would surely be crushed when they found out what had happened the next morning. Whoever did this should pay for their actions.

As soon as Squeekie was sure that it was safe to come out of his hiding spot, he decided to investigate the scene. First, he ventured to the cash register. Because the robber had used gloves, he was certain that they did not leave any fingerprints behind. Squeekie did not see any possible clues that might identify the robber. Next, he carefully ventured to the front door, careful to avoid the broken glass. As he was walking, something caught his eye near the front door. It was a square card with writing on it: a business card! The print on it read, "Kristy's Whistle Stop".

"Hmmm, so the culprit must work at Kristy's!" thought Squeekie. Now, he would just have to find a creative way to tell the store owners that. Aware that there was nothing else he could do to help solve the case right now, he strolled back to his cozy corner and drifted off.

The next day, Squeekie awoke to a high pitched scream.

"That must be the workers!" Squeekie assumed.

He leapt out of his corner and ran to the front of the office to see what was going on. His tiny heart was racing in fear of how the employees would react. The workers were simply standing there, staring at the broken glass in disbelief; one of them was even crying.

"Call 9-1-1!" she shouted.

After a few minutes, the police arrived at the bookstore. They scanned the bookstore to search for any clues first, and then proceeded to clean up the hazardous broken glass near the front of the store. Squeekie saw that they had found nothing and thought it was the perfect time to break out his secret weapon!

Carrying the business card in his mouth, Squeekie trotted to the front of the bookstore. He hopped up onto the counter and approached the concerned workers. Using his nose, he slid the small piece of paper towards them. At first they were confused

"What's this?" one of them wondered aloud.

"A business card?" another replied.

"Why in the world do you have this Squeekie?"

All Squeekie could do was continue to tap the card with his paw, but they clearly were not getting the clue. So, he decided to refer to the damaged cash register. Shaking his paw violently, he pointed to the broken register and then back to the business card over and over again.

"Are you saying that this card had something to do with the crime?"

Squeekie shook his head up and down frantically, relieved that they had finally realized the card's importance.

The workers picked up the card and examined it closely.

"It's from Kristy's up the road!" one exclaimed. "Squeekie, did the culprit leave this behind when he robbed our store?"

The silver cat nodded again, confirming the worker's suspicions.

"I'll give this to the authorities right away!" she proclaimed.

The cops looked at the card closely and thought of the possible ways they could handle the situation. In the end, they told the employees that they would gather all of the male workers and take them in for questioning. Taking the card with them, the police exited the building with promises to return tomorrow.

The rest of the day at the bookstore was slow and quiet. Squeekie and the workers were all very sad about the unfortunate circumstances. Only two customers came in and they quickly left after because of the state that the shop was in. At eight, the shop closed, and Squeekie took this opportunity to get a good night's sleep since last night was so crazy.

In the morning, the local police returned to the bookstore along with some guests. All of the male workers at Kristy's Whistle stop shuffled in one by one. They lined up in the front of the store by the cash register and waited for further instructions.

"Just thought we would show you who we were questioning before we actually began the process," a cop said.

Squeekie examined the line of men closely. He hadn't seen the robber's face clearly, but who knows, he might be able to identify him just by his figure. Sadly, quite a few of the suspects were tall and skinny, so there was no way to tell for sure who the culprit was. Then, Squeekie had a thought.

"The man who robbed the store broke through the glass with his right hand... The guilty party must have an injured hand!" Squeekie thought.

Quickly, Squeekie, ran over to the men and started to look at their hands. The first few suspects in line had no injuries, but a slender man in the middle of the line had bandages on his right hand! Squeekie dashed over to get a closer look.

"This has to be him!" Squeekie thought. "Now how do I get the others to realize that?"

At first, Squeekie just sat by his side, but no one noticed that he was even there. So, he decided to start jumping up and down to become noticeable.

"Squeekie, stop that!" one of the owners scolded.

Discouraged, Squeekie laid down on the ground and thought of ways to call out the robber.

"What if I point to his hand?"

The cat jumped back up and instead of hopping around, this time he hit the man's hand with his paw.

"Ouch! Get off of me you stupid cat!" yelled the man.

The police eyed the man closer and he seemed to notice the bandage.

"Where did you hurt your hand, sir?" the policeman questioned.

"Um it's just a blister from scooping ice cream," the man responded

"Would you mind removing your bandage then?"

"Uhh it shouldn't be removed for another week."

"That seems a bit excessive for a blister, don't you think?"

Reluctantly, the man removed his bandage which revealed cut up knuckles and large cuts all over the palm of his hand!

"Now's my chance!" Squeekie thought.

Squeekie ran over, grabbed the business card out of the cop's hand and set it in front of the prime suspect.

"Squeekie, is this the man who broke in the other night?" asked one of the workers.

Immediately, Squeekie shook his head up and down. They had finally figured it out!

"Come on, are you seriously gonna listen to a cat?" asked the culprit.

"Sir, you are the only one of these men with a cut up hand. Whoever broke in would have an injury from punching through the glass," stated the police officer.

The man looked around and then sighed.

"Alright, I did it. I needed some extra money to pay my friend back," confessed the man.

Squeekie smiled with joy, ecstatic that he finally helped the others solve the crime!

"You're gonna have to come with us down to the police office for further questioning." The police officer grabbed the man and began to take him out to his car. "The rest of you are free to go."

After five minutes, the cops and the suspects had cleared out of the store and everything seemed to be normal again.

"Squeekie, what would we do without you!" one of the workers exclaimed.

That day, Squeekie had more treats than he had in months,

and when he got out his Nancy Drew book before bed, he felt like just as much as a detective as she was.

Squeekie: Cat Detective

AUTHOR BIOGRAPHY

Lindsay Grubb is a senior at East Pennsboro High school. While she has not published any pieces before "Squeekie: Cat Detective", writing is one of her many hobbies along with running, singing, playing lacrosse, and reading. Lindsay hopes to major in either communications or political science when she departs for college next fall. In Mechanicsburg, Pennsylvania, Lindsay resides with her loving family.

Squeekie the Bookstore Cat

11

Squeekie and the Nine Lives

Donna Leiss

I was about to settle in for the night having had another glorious day at the bookstore. Lots of attention and pets from customers, adults and children alike, left me ready for sleep. Yet, after I finished cleaning myself, before hunkering down into my roost, something caught my ear. The sound of the humans. Singing, to be exact. But how could that be when Mother and my special bookstore humans had left for the night, turning out the lights and locking the door behind them? Curiosity overtook me, of course, and with a yawn and a stretch I bound from my perch.

I round the corner to the front of the store expecting to find a human there. One of my special humans who had forgotten something and come back, even though I did not hear the bell on the door, or a customer who had missed the closing cues distracted by the shelves upon shelves of books and was overlooked. Instead, I find no one. I continue on past the check-out counter towards the back room determined to find the source. My head swivels looking down each row. I hear the singing again, from behind me this time. Definitely a human female. I whip around and start back the other way, ears back and tail bristled.

A cry-hiss escapes my lips as I nearly jump out of my fur when someone above me says, "Sorry, Squeekie. I didn't mean to disturb you."

I look up, but only find the cages containing the temporary cats. Ones in need of a forever home. The largest and oldest, a grey tabby with a light lavender blue hue they call Violet, stares down at me.

"Hello!" she says giving me another start. She waves her paw at me with wide eyes and a cocked head as if I'm daft.

"You speak human?" I ask, the look of surprise still on my face.

"Well, yeah," she responds, as if a cat speaking human is no big deal. She goes on, "I don't do it in front of many humans though. It kind of freaks them out."

"You don't say," I respond.

"I saw you interact with your Mother and caretakers earlier and realized you understand human speak though. Sorry to interrupt your sleep. I thought a lullaby would soothe the younger ones fears about being in a cage and finding a home," Violet states, motioning to the other temporary cats in the cage next to hers, finishing the sentence in a whisper.

"You're not worried about finding a home?" I ask, my voice revealing the concern I have. The kittens and young cats find homes quickly, while the older felines wait a long time for someone to take them.

"Nope. I figure I will be out of here soon and into the right home. My ability to understand all humans and communicate with some helps. I've been around a long time. I'm on my last life, you know," she says.

"Last life?" I ask.

"Yes, my ninth."

I have heard people talk about cats having nine lives, but believed it was only part of human folklore. Violet assures me it is not, that all cats indeed have nine lives.

"Do you remember any of yours?" I ask, not yet quite believing her.

"Well, of course. Don't you?"

I take a few seconds to think about it, then tell her about the red-haired woman I lived with before coming here.

She shakes her head, "It seems that was before you got to the bookstore, but still this life. No, I am talking about when one life fades and you re-emerge into a new one." Seeing the confusion on my face Violet adds, "Let me tell you about my previous life with my owner, Sandy, and then you'll understand."

Squeekie and the Nine Lives

Sandy was a great mom to me, especially since I inserted myself into her life. I was drawn to her; she needed me and I also needed her, so I kept following her into the house until she relented. Sandy only saw herself as an overweight, homely doormat, and spinster and so that's how the rest of the world treated her. She allowed her co-workers, friends, and her own mother to insult her with hardly a peep. When her mother asked if she'd finally found a boyfriend or if it was still just her and "that cat", Sandy would reply pleasantly "Still me and Winkles." When her friends would emphasize she "didn't understand" when they spoke of their struggles with their kids, she'd smile and nod her head while her heart broke. When her co-workers teased her for being heavy and frumpy, she'd smile and blush wanting to hide under her desk. Instead of correcting her secret work crush when he'd notice her and say "Hello, Mandy" her only response was a meek "hello" and a smile, thankful he'd noticed her at all. I know all these things because she'd come home and ask me why didn't she say what she was thinking? Why didn't she tell her mother she wasn't incomplete without a man? Why didn't she tell her friends not having children did not make her an idiot or less than a woman? Why didn't she tell her vain, twiggy co-workers to shove it and then sit on them? And why, oh why, didn't she tell Jim her name was Sandy two years ago when he'd first gotten it wrong? Or maybe even Sandra to sound more confident. I would tell her over and over again to stand up for herself, to love herself the way I did, but all she heard were meows.

I would manage to comfort her by giving her kisses or allowing her to pet me, but this one night she was inconsolable and cried for hours. I kept tabs on the amount of wine and medicine she inhaled, whereas she did not and...

"I'm sorry. Winkles? Your name is Winkles?" I ask, laughing.

Violet shot me a look of contempt for the interruption before answering, "*Was,* Squeekie. It was her nickname for me. My full name was Periwinkle after my beautiful coloring," she says smugly. "May I continue?" she asks.

I motion with my paw for Violet to do so. At this, she rises up and acts out the rest of her story.

Suddenly, Sandy's eyelids closed like a roll top desk and she fell off the couch onto the floor. I meowed the loudest I have ever meowed, but Sandy didn't wake up. So, I did the only thing I knew. CPR. I'd seen it performed on TV. I jumped up and down on her chest like a child on a trampoline between takes of blowing into her mouth. My paws fixed on either side of her head. I was nose to nose with Sandy to give her another breath when I realized one of her eyes had opened. Wide. She was alive! Thank goodness, because I wasn't sure how much longer I could keep doing CPR. I told her as much and that time she actually understood me, which caused her to completely freak out. The near death experience had finally allowed her to hear me speaking.

It took hours for her to calm down and listen to me, accomplished by some gross vomiting (and people have the nerve to say a cat throwing up is the worst), a long shower, and a slap in the face by yours truly. I told her I loved her and she was not going to do this again. She had to gain some confidence and self-esteem. I informed her she acts like a dog when she needs to act like a cat. Dogs fetch when they're told, roll over in submission, lower their heads when humans aren't pleased with them, run and hide with their tail between their legs, and wag their tail and happily return to people who treat them harshly. That was Sandy to a T. Equally annoying to me was Sandy also acted like she lived with a dog. She expected me to greet her at the door after a long day alone in the house, and then wept because she didn't have anyone. What was I? Chopped liver? And I loved her no matter what, but she had let herself go. Dogs don't care what their owner looks like, but felines are not that forgiving.

I explained I was going to "catify" her. Teach her how to stop wallowing in useless self-pity, stand up for herself, and to be fearless and fierce. I was not pleased at all when Sandy's only response was she did not want to come across as "the B word". Scowling, I advised her "the B word" was a dog term and we would not speak of it again. I spent every moment of the long weekend schooling her in cat actions and reactions, including ignoring mean people, self-confidence, and how to get what you want out of life. I even taught her male attraction techniques so Jim would not only remember her name, he would not be able to forget her. We finished off her transformation with a make-over, including sleek clothes, a new mane, and her getting her claws, I mean, fingernails and toenails manicured and polished.

I sent Sandy off to work the next day with a "Go get 'em, tiger." I was pleased when she bounded in the door much earlier than normal with the largest smile on her face. Breathless, she grabbed me and kissed me before she detailed her day for me. She had walked in to work with her head held high like she owned the place and people responded with jaw-dropped stares and compliments. She gave her co-workers a piece of her mind with squinted eyes and hisses, her rear end swishing a warning like I had taught her. Sandy then darted into her boss, Mr. Fletcher's office, and demanded the bonus she was due and the raise she deserved. Feeling good, she hunted for Jim. She pretended to bump into him by accident before correcting him on her name, sounding like a long purr. Looking up at him with big eyes under long lashes, she secured a date with him. Acting cool and indifferent she sauntered away, imaginary tail flicked upright.

With each passing day Sandy became more self-assured, fulfilled, and content. She no longer dreaded being around people nor did she let them rule her. She demanded respect. Her nasty co-workers even became a bit afraid of her, which she liked- she had the power. She also grew to be as comfortable being alone, although that rarely occurred with Jim in her life. He chased after her like a dog. It was when I heard her caterwaul I knew it was my time to go. I did my job; Sandy didn't need me any longer. I took my leave from Sandy's life in the wee morning hours before she awoke. I could hear her cries for me as my stiff body lay there motionless. I hated to break her heart, but I knew it would heal in time and she would be fine without me. She and Jim buried me in the backyard with my favorite toy mouse.

Tears fill my eyes as Violet continues, "When the full moon was overhead, I was reanimated into this life, my ninth, and crawled out of the ground. I know I won't be able to do that after this life ends, but that is okay. I've had a lot of love and know I will in this life too." She pauses and looks at me. "Do you understand better now, Squeekie?"

I nod, unable to speak from the lump in my throat. Violet curls up in a big ball.

"I'm tired now, Squeekie. Good night, friend."

I too curl up for the night, only falling asleep trying to recall past lives and counting them. My sleep is fitful and I wake many times in a panic. Is this my last life?

The tinkling of the bell on the bookstore door startles me. It takes me a moment to realize it is morning. I find myself dashing to greet Mother and my special humans. I am so happy to still be in this life, but I also laugh at myself for acting like a dog. I look at them, and later the customers, with renewed vision- one of eternal affection and gratitude. I see Violet wave to me from a carrier at the hip of an elderly woman with kind eyes, and it's at that second I truly understand Violet's tale and all my fear dissipates. It makes no sense to live in the past or the future. The present, this life at the bookstore, is the only one that matters and I should live it to the fullest. I love it with all my heart. If this is to be my last life, there's nowhere else I'd rather spend it.

AUTHOR BIOGRAPHY

Donna Leiss has been in love with reading, writing, art, and music since she was a little girl. They all have played a key role in keeping her sane over the years - at least, as sane a writer can be. She has completed two year-long novel writing courses given by the Perry County Council of the Arts and had her short story "The Black Dress" published in 2017 in the anthology *Strange Magic*. She currently resides in Middletown, PA with her husband and two Siberian huskies, where she continues to create.

12

Squeekie's Big (Imaginary) Night

Joshua Short

The door opened and the humans came in. It is time to open for the day! Squeekie settled himself down between stacks of books. Even though this was one of his very favorite spots in the whole store (at least until it too is filled with books) the obligatory circling and pawing was not disregarded. Many centuries ago his ancestors did this to ensure there was not a predator lying in wait for an easy, sleepy, meal. Now –well some habits hang around for a looong time.

But sleep did not come. The store was quickly buzzing with excitement. Squeekie's people had been going through a pile of books that they had in the basement and something seemed to excite them. He really did not see what all of the fuss was about- it looked like an ordinary book to him. A bunch of faintly yellowed pages between two covers.

People are so very odd Squeekie thought. After all, it is just a book. The one lady seemed very pleased and kept saying over and over "I had no idea that THIS was in the basement" "Imagine, a FIRST EDITION of Mansfield Park, and signed too."

Eventually the horrid book that caused so much excitement was moved into the locked case where the rarest books go.

But of course Squeekie still was unable to relax. The book was apparently so special that animated conversations about it needed to take place on the phone. "With all of this hubbub I'll never sleep" thought Squeekie sadly.

At last everyone left and all was silent. Finally solitude filled the air. Though only sounds were the traffic on the highway and the trainyard in the distance.

The store had closed hours before, all was quiet and darkness had recently filled the sky. It was one of Squeekie's favorite times of day because it was so quiet- many creatures had gone to bed, creatures of the night were just waking. It was still and quiet almost anything could be heard.

But what was heard was something totally new. An odd cross between a squeak and a scratch came to Squeekie's alert ears. He slowly padded to the front door to see what it may be. In the dim light he saw a man, dressed all in black, stealthily and fully cut a hole in the glass door. Squekie knew he had to act fast!

He ran to his bowl and dipped his tail into his water. This he mopped generously onto the bare floor right inside the door. It took several trips because his tail did not hold very much water but it worked like a charm. The man finished cutting the hole and reached in to twist the lock. Of course this earned him 5 deep scratches courtesy of Squeekie's razor sharp claws.

The enraged man charged through the door with thoughts of accosting Squeekie in his mind. He slipped on the wet floor and slid right into a bookshelf! Of course the heavy shelf tipped over spilling its burden onto the robber. Squeekie had to look away it looked so painful. To see it was just too much to bear. The sound alone was appalling.

Slowly the man got up and brushed himself off. Squeekie was not done. He vaulted off the top of a nearby shelf landing square on the man's head. The confused man tripped over the pile of books at his feet and fell once again. He rolled over a few times, gaining a bit of distance between himself and the scattered books.

Squeekie darted into hiding and from his safe vantage point he surveyed the work he had done so far. True, things were in a bit of a disarray but to his credit, the man had barely made it past the entrance of the store. He was at least 5 feet from the desk, but who knows if that is even the goal. Actually Squeekie could not think of anything in the entire store to warrant such an act. A robbery was daring and a great way to get into very big trouble.

Annika finally showed up. Slinking up to Squeekie she asked

Squeekie's Big (Imaginary) Night

"What are you doing?" "About time you came to help" Squeekie hissed "I called your name when I first sensed trouble".

Annika adopted a look of nonchalance and dignity, a look only some cats and certainly no people can portray. Squeekie simply looked at her in a hard way. Being a Siamese, he knew that he deserved the respect and deference Annika thought she was entitled to.

The man slowly crawled to his feet, but not without hesitation and a look around in the dim light. The two cats had communicated with just a few glances and it was decided that the fellow certainly deserved some love!

As he walked toward the older books the two weaved in and out of his legs, rubbing them and purring loudly. Disoriented, the man soon stumbled and fell once again, although it was the gentlest landing he had that night.

By now Squeekie had figured out what his goal was. People are so funny thought Squeekie, all the fuss over some book and now a robber had decided to try to steal it. Although Squeekie had no clue why it was so important to so many people, he knew that it had to be protected. After all, a few customers had called him a guard cat! He directed Annika to stand right in the middle of the isle that the man had to walk down.

The robber slowly made his way toward the corner. The dim light illuminated things a bit but Annika was around the corner, in the shadows. She was at the perfect spot and when the man's leg collided with her fur he faltered. Squeekie was on top of the nearest case and he swatted at the man's balding head. The two had pushed some rather thick books into the aisle and combined with all the distractions the man had no chance. "Ow" he yelled and, off balance, he fell to his hands and knees.

Squeekie rubbed up against the fallen man's face. Although to the observer it would seem that he was marking the man by pushing his face into his fallen prey's face he actually had a more aggressive motivation. He hoped to introduce some furry irritants to the man's eyes.

But fortune was with the two heroic cats- the man's breathing was always slightly funny gradually turned to a definite wheeze.

The robber was terribly allergic to cats! Entering the bookstore caused a bit of distress but Squeekie's nuzzling caused even more of a reaction than he could have hoped. The two felines almost felt sorry for the miscreant as he was reduced from the formidable opponent he had seemed to be when he stealthily entered the store to a bruised, wheezing shadow with red puffy eyes.

The man crawled to the door muttering something about completing his Jane Austin collection not being worth all this. He also made several remarks which made it clear he was not a fan of cats. He was certainly deserving of all that I have done to him, thought Squeekie.

The bell tinkled as the man made his exit. He was not as smooth as he was in entering. Squeekie had won! With a yawn Annika said that she needed to go back to bed. She also indicated that she had done most of the work. She was so entitled thought Squeekie. No matter what the situation was, Annika always managed to manipulate it in such a way that the attention was focused on her! To be fair, she was helpful tonight, if a bit delayed in arriving. On any given day she was decent, even good company. But of course, she may never know the rather high regard Squeekie held her in. *With her head inflated even more she might become intolerable*, thought Squeekie with a cringe.

But what a mess, he thought while surveying the damage. Books were everywhere and the floor was nice and wet. *Well, the water will dry and when the people see how much of a hero I am, they won't mind the mess!*

But when they were coming in it was odd that nobody commented on the hole in the glass. Or the door being unlocked. Or the tipped over bookcase with books everywhere. Actually, Squeekie could not even see it now. Funny how the daylight makes things look entirely different. Some things were hard to understand- if they could be understood at all. Squeekie thought that perhaps this was one of those things that could only be understood if it were thought about in depth for some time.

But Squeekie *knew* he was a hero. He had single handedly foiled a robbery that would have most certainly been of ghastly

Squeekie's Big (Imaginary) Night

proportions! He knew that the skritches he received from the staff this morning were more deserved than they had ever been before.

He circled the area three times, pawed around, and settled in to take his well-deserved nap.

AUTHOR BIOGRAPHY

Joshua Short lives in Hershey, PA with his wife Jenni and cats, Catrina, BobCat, and Selma. He also has an adopted dog, Casey. He likes tinkering with tractors as well fixing nearly everything else. Joshua enjoys reading, especially books that have cats as crime-solving characters.

13

Squeekie and the Goddess

Jennifer Woodings

Long ago, man worshiped cats and this is something they have never forgotten...

From his usual afternoon perch in the sunny front window that faced the highway, Squeekie listened to the sounds of the bookstore as the people went about their business, footsteps slapping against the concrete then turning to echoing thuds as they crossed onto the wooden floor at the front of the store, the click of the keys at the computer behind the desk, and conversations waxing and waning as people passed through the store. Things were relatively quiet for the moment since most of the people were busy with some project in the back room that seemed to involve a lot of dust and rattling of the book cart and Annika, having taken her cue from Squeekie, was napping in a place of her own preference. The front door beeped announcing a person's entry into the air conditioned interior of the store and the hot breeze that accompanied them carried a sweet, dry, musky smell that made his whiskers twitch in recognition though he couldn't remember having ever smelled it before. Startled by the sensation he stretched and made his way toward the entry way to investigate its source. A woman he had never seen before was standing at the front counter and talking with Michelle about some books that had been left to her by a relative.

"I'm not really sure what all is there but they were really into folklore and world mythology and I just don't have the space, or interest, to be honest, to keep them." the woman finished as Squeekie leaped up onto the counter. Her hand automatically reached out and began scratching him between the ears as she waited for Michelle's response. "Were you looking to just donate them or...."

The woman cut Michelle off before she could finish, "No, I wasn't looking for any kind of credit or anything. I just wanted to get them to somewhere where they'll be appreciated." Squeekie pushed his head harder against the woman's fingers while rumbling a contented purr as Michelle thanked the woman and told her where to set the boxes in the entryway. With her deal made the woman gave Squeekie one last scratch behind the ears before moving away from the counter to go bring in the boxes.

As the woman neatly stacked the boxes by the display in the entry Squeekie sat and sniffed at the air, trying to recapture the scent that had caught his attention but could no longer find any trace of it. The boxes themselves seemed ordinary enough, though he would have to investigate them more thoroughly later once Michelle had left for the night. She always seemed a bit nervous when he was in the entry during the day and he had no wish to be sprayed again today. Remembering where she had gotten him earlier he checked his back and realized that he still had an odd part in his fur from where he had gotten wet and settled in for a quick bath to put things to rights. Soon all thoughts of the unknown but familiar smell faded from his mind and the remainder of the day passed uneventfully until Michelle closed up for the evening.

With the store closed, Squeekie made a circuit of the store to ensure that all was as it should be before joining Annika on the front counter. Her tail was twitching with excitement when he got there and there was a curious glint in her eyes. "Did you smell it?" she asked as soon as he had landed next to her. "Did I smell what, Annika?" he muttered only half paying attention as he tucked his paws under his chest. "You know. IT! The smell she brought with her. It was old and warm and felt good in my whiskers," her tail twitched faster in agitation. Squeekie thought for a moment then shifted to turn and clean the fur on his back again. He usually found it was better to have a definite answer before speaking when Annika was in this kind of mood and grooming gave him a chance to think. Annika sat quietly staring at him, impatient for his response.

After a few licks, Squeekie thought of something, straightened up and looked at Annika, "Do you mean that lady who left all the boxes in the entry? Yeah, I smelled it. It seemed so familiar, but I know I've never smelled anything like it. Maybe it was something in one of the boxes? I wanted to take a look at them earlier but couldn't really get near." He hopped down from the counter and made his way back out to the entry with Annika only a few steps behind him. The two cats circled the stack of boxes in opposite directions occasionally poking a nose under a box lid to get a better smell of its contents. They were greeted by the all too familiar aroma of old books and cardboard that was common around the store. "I could've sworn that smell came from one of these boxes," Squeekie complained as he leaped up on top of the shorter of the two stacks and sat with his tail wrapped around his toes. Annika, for her part, continued to circle the stacks trying to recapture the smell that had teased her subconscious all day.

Suddenly, the stack Squeekie had perched on shifted as the cardboard box at the bottom gave out at one corner and began to tear open. Annika hopped back as a trickle of sand poured from the tear in the box and over her front paws. "Why would someone bring us a box of sand?" she wondered aloud as she daintily shook first one paw then the other to dislodge the grains of sand from her fur. As the grains scattered across the floor an almost intoxicating smell filled the air in the entryway sending electric waves of excitement rippling through both cats. Squeekie hopped lightly down from his perch, landing next to Annika and sniffing at the spill of sand. A glint of something gold caught his attention and he moved closer to examine it. "I think that lady must've dropped a ring or something in this box, Annika." Squeekie posited as he gently batted the sand away from the shining object to reveal a small alabaster figure of a cat with a golden gorget around its neck.

As the two cats stared in fascination at the figure a dry desert wind rose around them whisking the grains of sand into the air and spinning them like a miniature tornado. Squeekie and Annika crouched low to the floor, their ears flat against their heads and eyes closed to slits as they backed away from the whirlwind of sand that seemed grow denser before them. Soon the two cats found themselves backed into the corner by the front door of the shop watching in awe as the growing sandstorm spiraled ever more tightly until they could almost make out the form a person standing at its center. A rumbling growl poured forth from the funnel of sand as two bright turquoise eyes opened within its depths and focused on the cats. In an instant, the wind died and the last grains of sand fell to the floor revealing a slender woman with alabaster skin. Her long sheath-like dress of undyed linen made the colorfully bejeweled ornaments that she wore stand out in stark contrast. Her kohl-lined eyes stared down at the two cats from the mane-less head of a lioness. Her magnificent appearance was ruined in a moment by the yawn that stretched her jaws wide only a moment later.

"Do not be afraid my children, no harm will come to you from my hand." the goddess purred as she stretched both arms behind her back. "My apologies for startling you. It has been far too long since I last manifested. I fear I may have been a bit too dramatic with my entrance," she continued as she tried, and failed, to stifle a second yawn. Squeekie and Annika relaxed ever so slightly and moved a few steps forward away from the wall. "We accept your apology, my Lady, though your form is fairly intimidating to cats as small as we are," Squeekie replied hesitantly, not wishing to offend the goddess. "Intimidating? What..," the goddess began before reaching out and grabbing a small mirror that appeared by her hand and gazing into it. "I see what you mean! A lioness once again. That *would* intimidate. Is this better?" she finished as she slid the mirror away from her face to reveal her head was now that of a, somewhat oversized, house cat. Satisfied with the change she released the mirror which promptly disappeared back to where ever she had summoned it from. "You do us great honor, my Lady, to change your appearance for us," Squeekie replied as he moved forward to rub against the goddess's legs. Unimpressed by her

Squeekie and the Goddess

companion's show of affection, Annika lay down with her back partially turned toward the goddess and began to work at removing the last stubborn grains of sand from her paws.

"Have I done something to upset your friend? Perhaps, interrupted your date?" the goddess queried as she bent down to pick up Squeekie and cradle him against her shoulder. "I wish," Squeekie muttered under his breath as Annika froze in mid-lick to turn and glare at the goddess, her tail twitching in agitation. "No," Squeekie continued louder, "that's just the way Annika is. She's really very nice, once she gets to know you. Honestly, I think she's just jealous. You're quite beautiful, my Lady, and she's used to being admired for her beauty." Annika sniffed indignantly in response. "You make me sound like a vain little beast! I can't help it that everyone loves how soft and long my fur is." she paused to lick a paw and use it to put a stray wisp of fur back behind her ear. "It's a burden really, being this beautiful. But it's my curse to bear I suppose," she finished thoughtfully as she resumed her grooming in earnest this time. An amused look crossed the goddess's face as she watched Annika go about her toilet for a moment. "A curse, is it? Well, I would not want it to be said that I was unable to protect my children from such discomfort," the goddess said as she stepped forward and reached down to stroke Annika's back. With a gasp of surprise, Squeekie leaped down from the goddess's arms and darted behind her legs. A wave of golden light poured over Annika moving from the top of her head to the tip of her tail illuminating each and every one of the luxuriant strands of fur in her coat. When the light faded Squeekie could see that Annika was now completely bald!

"Now, now, Squeekie. It's not polite to stare." the goddess gently chided him with a hint of laughter in her voice. Squeekie's mouth hung open for a moment longer in shock before he closed it abruptly to choke off the laughter he felt bubbling up within him. He knew that if he laughed now Annika would never forgive him. "What?! What are you staring at Squeekie?" Annika inquired intensely, not yet noticing the change to her appearance. "You're p...p...p..pi..." Squeekie stuttered trying to get the word out without laughing. "I'm what? Pretty? Perfect? Spit it out!" Annika ordered.

"YOU'RE PINK!" Squeekie blurted out before dissolving into fits of laughter. "Pink? What on earth has gotten into you, Squeekie!" Annika replied as she turned to resume her grooming and her eyes took in her, now hairless, appearance. "My fur! What? How? What did you do to my beautiful fur?!" she cried despairingly at the goddess as she jumped to her feet and turned every which way trying to get a better look at her changed appearance. "You said your beauty was a burden, a curse. So I freed you from it. Was that not what you wanted?" the goddess answered with only a hint of laughter in her voice. "NO! No, it wasn't! I would never want to be rid of my beautiful fur! Now I'm nothing but some hairless pink freak! No one will want to pet me or love me now. I'm hideous." Annika wailed as she tried to curl into a ball to hide her nakedness.

Squeekie choked back his laughter and took a deep breath to compose himself before speaking. "I'm sorry Annika. I shouldn't have laughed like that, it was just the shock of seeing you change like that. It's really not that bad. Just think, you'll stay so much cooler in the summer now and won't have to worry about your fur getting matted." He stepped out from behind the goddess and went over to lean his head gently against Annika's. "Would it make you feel better if I was bald too?" he whispered caringly. The goddess watched in fascination as Annika lifted her eyes to meet Squeekie's. "You would really do that for me? Even after all the times I've bossed you around?" she asked, her voice catching in her throat. Squeekie sat back in shock, "Of course I would Annika! You're my friend." Annika sat up, shifted a little closer to Squeekie then leaned against him. "Oh, Squeekie. What did I ever do to deserve a friend like you? Thank you, you have no idea how much your offer means to me. But, I can't let you do that." Annika sighed. "Nor can I." the goddess interrupted. "I can see now why so many of my children mention you in their prayers, Squeekie." With a slow blink of the goddess's bright turquoise eyes, Annika's coat was restored to its former appearance. "There are few who would give so unselfishly of themselves in order to comfort a friend, but you do so without hesitation. That is a great gift."

With an expansive wave of her arm, the goddess sent a

cascade of multicolored light washing over the bookstore. As it passed bits of light detached themselves and took on the shapes of a variety of cats of different ages and descriptions. Some were familiar to Squeekie and Annika as cats who had been fostered here in the bookstore, others were complete strangers and still others seemed to come from other times and places far way. The one thing they all had in common was that their form was filled with an otherworldly light. Once formed, each cat went bounding about the store as if it were the greatest playground that ever existed. Though they often ran across the tops of bookshelves or over desktops, not a single book or piece of paper was disturbed by their passing. Squeekie turned to say something to Annika only to immediately forget it upon seeing the same unearthly glow radiating from her as well. Looking down he realized that he also was glowing, though the only difference he felt was a sense of well-being and joy. The last sparkles of light returned to the goddess obscuring his view of her for just a moment and when they had cleared he could see that she had now taken the form of a cat herself.

"I am sorry for having a bit of fun at your expense, Annika, and I humbly beg you to forgive me. It has been far too long since I have gone among my children and I could not resist the temptation." the goddess trilled good-naturedly as she approached the two cats with tail held high. "That's alright, I kind've brought it upon myself by not watching what I said to a goddess. Do you forgive me my rudeness, my Lady?" Annika asked with chagrin. "Of course! I could never stay mad at one of my children for responding in the way that I might in one of my vainer moments. For tonight, let us not be as mother and children, but rather friends and equals. With that said," the goddess reached out a paw and batted at Squeekie's nose, "TAG! You're it!"

The rest of the night passed in a multicolored blur as the dozens of glowing cats romped about the store with their goddess. Old friends reunited, and friends yet to be met for the first time, though none of them would ever be able to clearly remember the events of the night. For the rest of their lives, all present would have dreams of sparkling forms of multicolored light chasing each other about like fireworks gone berserk and would awaken from those dreams feeling renewed and loved. As the night wound its way down toward dawn each shimmering cat would settle down to sleep and when next someone would think to look for them they would be found to have disappeared as easily as they had appeared. Just before dawn the goddess lay down on top of one of the boxes in the entryway and was joined by Squeekie and Annika.

A yawn once more stretched the goddess's jaws wide as the three cats settled down on the battered box lid. "My children, no, my friends, you have truly given me a night to remember! For that I thank you both," the goddess trilled tiredly as Squeekie and Annika purred contentedly at her sides. "Before this night is over I have one last gift to give you both," she continued as she shifted to lick first Squeekie's then Annika's forehead right between their eyes. "The two of you now bear my mark and blessing. Should you ever need me I will be there." Sleepily the two cats murmured their thanks as the goddess's form shimmered once more to that of the lioness-headed woman. Her hands gently stroked both cats as they let out little snores of contentment in their sleep. Quietly she bent down and picked up the alabaster cat figure with its golden gorget and placed it high on a dusty unused shelf above the entryway before fading away on a dry desert wind.

AUTHOR BIOGRAPHY

Jennifer Woodings was born and raised in Marysville, Pennsylvania. Her parents instilled a love of reading into her at an early age that has carried her through her life. Her love of books lead her to start writing in the hopes that she could give someone else the same joy that her favorite authors have brought her over the years. She studied English Writing at Edinboro University. She lives in her childhood home with her Mother, and a diminutive feline named Sage. This is her first published fiction work.

Squeekie the Bookstore Cat

14

The Druken Comic Book Monkeys vs. Squeekie

Brian Koscienski & Chris Pisano

"Do you guys even know why you're here?"

"Bacon," Brian replied.

"Bacon," Chris answered.

Michelle, the well-respected owner of Cupboard Maker Books, slapped her palm against her forehead. She ran her hand down her face as if trying to pull all the bad thoughts out of her head. "Seriously? The event is called Books, Bonding, and Bacon, remember? You guys set up a table for your books and you bond with the community."

"Bacon," Chris said.

"Community?" Brian asked.

Michelle sighed. "Yes, community. You know – neighbors. People. Camaraderie. Socially acceptable human interaction."

Brian and Chris looked at each other as if Michelle spoke to them in a foreign language. They shrugged and looked back at Michelle with lost puppy-dog eyes.

"Did you idiots at least bring books?"

Brian held out a dozen copies of *The Drunken Comic Book Monkeys in: Scary Tales of Scariness* while Chris presented twelve copies of *The Drunken Comic Book Monkeys in: Sciencey Tales of Science Fiction.*

Brow flattened and lips pursed, Michelle mumbled, "You guys think you're so meta, don't you?"

"We try," Brian said.

"Bacon," Chris said.

"Fine!" Michelle snapped. "I'll go start the bacon. It'll be done in ten minutes, so stay out of trouble." She rolled her eyes and stormed off in a huff.

Putting their books on the table, Brian said, "This is why she likes me more."

Chris fussed with the books, trying to arrange them in a pleasant display. "Why? Because I'm succinct and don't waste her valuable time with superfluous hyperbole? I'm not a sesquipedalian individual like you."

"Yeah, that's me. Using big words for no reason at all. Yep, totally me," Brian replied, sarcasm dripping from his words. Noticing a small puddle forming on the corner of the tablecloth, he realized it wasn't truly sarcasm dripping from him, but rather the thoughts of bacon kicking his saliva glands into high gear.

In an effort to hide the drool spot, he shifted the tablecloth and caused the stacks of books to move an inch and a half. This, of course, rankled Chris. "Dude! You moved the books that I've been working hard to arrange in a pleasant display."

"Yeah? Well, this is how Squeekie wants them."

"Squeekie? What are you even talking about?"

As if on cue, Squeekie, the guardian lion of the store (in Siamese cat form, that is) jumped onto the table and rubbed against one of the stacks, knocking it over creating a festive fanning effect with the books. Brian gestured to Squeekie with both hands and said, "See? Squeekie wants it this way."

"I highly doubt that."

Squeekie meowed.

Brian leaned close to Chris and attempted to whisper, but it came out more like a yell, "I think Squeekie is after our bacon."

Chris waved his hands about as if shooing away an insect. "You're louder than an erupting volcano, and twice as terrifying. Of course Squeekie wants our bacon. He's a cat and cats love bacon. But he's not getting any of mine."

"Well, he's not getting of mine, either, unless he finds a way to distract us."

The cat meowed again and then jumped from the table. Confused, Brian and Chris followed Squeekie as he weaved his way among the shelves of the bookstore. Finally reaching the far corner of the store, Squeekie walked under a small archway covered with brush bristles, making sure they brushed the entire length of his back and tail. Purring, he turned around and repeated the process.

"A backscratcher. Why would he show us a backscratcher?" Chris asked. "Do you think he wants us to pet him?"

"Dude, you know very well that no living creature wants us to touch them. I think he's just showing off that he has cool toys and we don't."

"Well, that's mean."

"Yeah." Brian started to pout as he looked around, trying to determine if he could turn any part of the store into an ersatz backscratcher. He then found something better. "Oooooh, look at this."

"It's one of Squeekie's walkways."

Brian ran to the plank of wood spanning from the top of one bookshelf to another. "It is, but the bottom of it is line with some kind of felt or velvet."

"Felvet?"

"Exactly!"

"So?"

"Watch!" Brian ducked down and positioned himself under the walkway. Carefully, he stood until his head touched the felvet. Still crouched, he walked the length of the board, from one set of shelves to the other, his head sliding along the felvet. "Oooooh, that feels so good against my bald head."

"Hey! I have a bald head, too! I wanna try."

"You're too short."

"No I'm not!" Determined to prove his writing partner wrong, Chris positioned himself under the walkway and stood on his toes. Flapping his arms to keep his balance, he wobbled from one end of the walkway to the other, his head barely grazing along the felvet. "See? I can touch! I'm tall enough to ride this ride!"

"You're not doing it right! This is how you do it." Brian did another lap of gliding his head against the felvet.

Chris took exception and repeated the process, still flapping.

"I'm faster!"

The men continued to run back and forth, slapping each other as they went along.

"I'm smarter!"

"I'm more elegant!"

"I'm better!"

"I'm prettier!"

One slap too many, the men knocked each other off balance, and both crashed into one of the shelves, knocking the walkway to the ground.

The two stood and stared at their mess, befuddled at how it came to be. Before they could burst into argument, Squeekie meowed to get their attention. The cat led and they blindly followed, all the way back to the front of the store. Once there, Squeekie walked around the counter. After a few seconds, a small ball – plastic and filled with tiny, aromatic leaves – rolled along the floor from behind the counter. Brian picked it up and sniffed it.

"Eeeeeew!" Chris crinkled his nose and furrowed his brows. "Do you always randomly sniff mysterious cat toys?"

Brian inhaled again. "I do when they're filled with hops."

"Hops! I wanna sniff!" Chris reached for the ball. Brian pulled it away, but having the coordination of a one-legged giraffe, he dropped it. Both men watched as the ball rolled down an aisle of books.

"Mine!" Brian yelled as he launched his flabby, out-of-shape body after it.

"Mine!" Chris lunged for the ball as well, body equally flabby and out-of-shape, just shorter.

Scrabbling along the ground, the men bounced from one shelf to the other while swatting at the ball. They gained and lost ground equally, the ball rolling sadistically just out of their reach. Brian elbowed Chris in the shoulder as they turned one corner; Chris kneed Brian in the hip when they turned the next corner. Alas, neither man could claim to be the victor as the ball rolled under one of the large shelves.

"Where's the ball go?" Chris asked, huffing and puffing on his hands and knees.

Panting, laying on his side, Brian answered, "Under the shelf there. Right where the red dot is."

"This red dot?" As Chris pointed to it, the little red dot moved a foot to the right. He aimed his index finger at it again, but it moved another foot to the right. "Hey! Why does it keep moving?"

"I don't know," Brian answered. "Hit it."

Chris tried. He slapped his hand on the floor where the red dot had been, missing as it jumped three feet to the left.

"You suck at this," Brian said as we strode over to the red dot and stepped on it. "See how easy that was?"

He missed as well, the dot now mere inches from his foot.

Chris stood and elbowed Brian out of the way. Putting the full weight of his body into it, he brought his foot down on the dot. "Here, I got this."

He did not get the dot. Both men watched as the dot danced in small circles while it made its way up the wall. Once the dot reached eye level, Chris swung after it, but missed. The dot now moved horizontally across the wall, avoiding Brian's hands with ease. Chris tried smacking at it again, but the red dot continued to move. Without warning, the dot went in the opposite direction, skimming along the wall even faster than before. Trying to anticipate its movements, Chris slapped both hands on the wall to no avail. Eyes widening with anticipation, Brian timed his hits perfectly, yet somehow still missed. Then the dot moved further up the wall.

Chris jumped and used both hands to swat at it. Even Brian had to stand on his toes to reach it. The dot angled downward, moving even faster than before. Whack, whack, Chris hit the wall with his hands. Smack, smack, Brian followed. Almost as if feeding off the men's collective incompetence, the elusive dot picked up speed.

Whack, whack.

Smack, smack.

Miss, miss.

The men moved apart, Brian claiming the left side of the wall while Chris guarded the right. In big looping circles, the dot scooted from one side of the wall to the other.

Whack, whack.

Smack, smack.

Miss, miss.

Panting and sweating, the men pawed at the dot whenever it got close to them, watched with rapt fascination whenever it was away from them. Their attacks became more frenzied, their hits more intense. Finally, the dot stopped moving. Right between the two men.

They released a battle cry and pounced, a furious attempt to stop the madness. The madness did end – with the hollow coconut sound of two empty heads colliding. The men slid down the wall, finishing in an unconscious heap of stupidity.

Michelle walked around the corner with a tray of bacon in her hands. "Okay, guys, I have your—" She cut herself short when she noticed the mess on the floor. "What have you two morons done this time?"

No answer.

She sighed, the involuntary reaction to the frustration of dealing with Brian and Chris, and walked to the front of the store to find Squeekie sitting on the checkout counter with a laser pointer in his mouth. Smiling, Michelle set the bacon on the counter and took the laser pointer. Petting him, Michelle said, "What are you doing with this thing? Oh well, I made bacon for the guys, but it doesn't seem like they want any, so it's all yours."

Squeekie purred.

Life was good.

AUTHOR BIOGRAPHY

Brian Koscienski & Chris Pisano skulk the realms of south, central Pennsylvania. Brian developed a love of writing from countless hours of reading comic books and losing himself in the worlds and adventures found within their colorful pages. In tenth grade, Chris was discouraged by his English teacher from reading H.P. Lovecraft, and being a naturally disobedient youth he has been a fan ever since. They have logged many hours writing novels, stories, articles, comic books, reviews, and the occasional bawdy haiku. During their tenure as a writing duo, they even started Fortress Publishing, Inc., a micro-press publishing company responsible for the *Drunken Comic Book Monkeys* short story collections and the *TV Gods* anthologies.

Squeekie the Bookstore Cat

15

A Friend Like Squeekie

Melissa Ford

Squeekie saw the lady when she walked in, but he didn't approach her until she sat down in the aisle. It had been a slow day and he was sleepy so he didn't want to chase anybody around the store, but when she sat down that meant there was a lap for Squeekie! He didn't always like to sit in laps, but people didn't always sit on the floor either, and Squeekie decided to take advantage of the situation. Maybe the lady just wanted a better look at what was on the lower shelves, but Squeekie thought she would like a visit from him while she was there. After all, who wouldn't want to hang out with the store mascot? Squeekie knew everybody loved him, so she would love him too, for sure!

The lady didn't notice Squeekie approach at first, but she smiled when she saw him and that made Squeekie happy. He liked it when people were happy, and he liked to make them feel that way. It made him feel important to help people. She hadn't been smiling before. She actually looked really sad when she first walked in, like she had been having a bad day. Squeekie thought maybe the lady had come to the bookstore to find an escape from her bad day. Books were a good escape, Squeekie knew.

The humans talked all the time about how they could "get lost in a book" and recommended books to each other so they could share being lost in that good way. Sometimes being lost was bad, like if a cat would get outside of the store, because it isn't always safe for a cat to be outside. Squeekie knew the humans didn't want him to get outside and get lost somewhere; they wanted him to stay inside and be safe. But lost outside for a cat is different from lost in a book for a human. Squeekie was a smart cat and he knew there was a difference, even though it was the same word. Bookstore cats learn a lot about words, if they are clever and pay attention, and Squeekie was a very clever cat and always listened to the conversations happening around him.

Squeekie sat with the lady for a little while while she pulled a few books from the shelf and paged through them. She was trying to decide if these books were good places for her to get lost, Squeekie knew. He watched people shop for books a lot. He hoped she would find some that would make her feel happy. There were a lot of books in the store for her to choose from, so he was sure she would find something she would like very much. The lady pet Squeekie gently and called him a good boy, and he liked that. He knew he was a good boy, but it was always nice to hear someone say so. Squeekie nuzzled the lady so she would know she was a good lady. She probably already knew that, but if she had been having a bad day, it would be even more important to remind her.

After a few minutes Squeekie climbed out of her lap and investigated her purse. He loved bags almost as much as he loved attention. Every bag was a new mystery, and it seemed like everybody carried one, so there was always something interesting for him to explore! It was a small bag so he couldn't get inside it, but that didn't keep him from trying. Trying to get in the purse made the lady smile again, even though she pulled the bag a little way away from him to stop his exploration. She called Squeekie silly and told him he couldn't fit in her purse. Squeekie tried to tell her that he wasn't silly, he was just having fun, but humans were always bad at knowing what Squeekie was trying to tell them. She asked if Squeekie was trying to come home with her by stowing away in her bag. Now the lady was the one being silly! Squeekie told her that his home was the store. He was always happy for people to come visit him there, but he wasn't going to go home with anybody because he already had a wonderful home that he loved. But there were other cats there who needed homes! Did she want to meet them?

But of course the lady didn't understand what Squeekie said

A Friend Like Squeekie

and she just smiled and pet him again. She put away the books she didn't want and took the one she chose up to the counter. Squeekie followed her partway there but stopped near Annika, who had been watching them from the end of another aisle. The lady paid for her book and waved goodbye to Squeekie when she left, giving him another smile. It was very satisfying to know he had made her day better just by being there!

"Why do you always get so close to the humans?" Annika asked him.

"Why wouldn't I?" he answered. "They love me! And they'd love you too if you got close to them. It makes them happy to spend time with me, and that makes me happy too. And this lady was sad, but now she's not! I helped her, and now I have a new friend. Don't you think that's nice?"

Annika made a little noise, like she understood what he was saying but didn't really agree. Squeekie understood – Annika hadn't been at the store as long as he had, and she had different feelings than he did. He was used to being around lots of people all the time and he loved it. Annika's life before coming to live at the store had been different and quieter, so she wasn't used to being around a lot of people, and she didn't always like the attention. Squeekie didn't know what it was like to not love attention, but he respected Annika's feelings. Even though they had different experiences and felt different ways, they could still be friends. Bookstores were full of different opinions and ways of thinking, and that was a good thing! It would be sad if nobody was ever different, and if nobody ever tried to learn from those differences. That was something else Squeekie had learned by being a bookstore cat.

Over the next several weeks, the lady came back a few more times. She always made sure to spend some time with Squeekie on each visit, and he was glad to see her, even if she could be a little silly sometimes and didn't really understand him when he talked. She was always kind, and that was important. Squeekie knew that you don't have to speak the same language to be nice to someone. He thought she seemed happier on these visits than when she came the first time, and that made Squeekie happy. He knew he was doing a good job when people were happy and came back.

Squeekie noticed that Annika paid attention when the lady came again. She watched the lady and how she was so nice to Squeekie. And Squeekie saw how Annika got just a little bit closer each time she watched. She didn't approach too closely, and she always ducked around the corner when the lady got up to walk around. The lady noticed Annika but didn't chase after her. The lady could tell that Annika wouldn't like to be treated the same way Squeekie did, and the lady was respecting that and letting Annika have space. For somebody who couldn't understand cat words, the lady seemed pretty good at understanding cat actions.

Squeekie started to spend a little less time with the lady on her visits, just in case Annika didn't want to get too close while he was around. He knew that it could be hard to try something new and he wanted Annika to not be embarrassed if she wanted to change a little bit. It was okay for her to not want to be close to people, but it was okay for her to want to try it, too. It would be okay if she changed her mind, or if she didn't, but she had to be given the chance to change. Squeekie had learned that from being at the bookstore too.

One day Squeekie didn't approach the lady at all. He was very comfy laying in the sunshine, so even though he saw her come in, he wasn't in a rush to visit with her. He knew the lady would stay for a while, and he would find her later before she left, or she could find him if she wanted. It was never too hard to find Squeekie if you knew where to look.

The lady didn't sit down in the aisle that day, but while she was looking at books on a high shelf, she felt something very soft and fluffy gently brush her leg. She looked down and smiled at Annika, and started to crouch down a little. The lady moved her hand down very slowly, because she didn't want to startle Annika. Annika tapped her head against the lady's extended fingers and walked away. Not too far away, though. The lady stood back up the whole way, smiled again, and told Annika she was a good girl.

Annika liked that. She knew that she was a good girl, but it was always nice to hear someone say so.

A Friend Like Squeekie

It was okay if she wanted to be around people. It was okay if she didn't. It was okay if she only wanted to be around people just a little bit and only sometimes. It was okay if how she felt was different every single day. Annika had learned that from being a bookstore cat. Bookstore cats learn a lot about life, if they are clever and pay attention, and especially if they have a friend like Squeekie, who will let them be themselves, even if that means changing a little sometimes.

Melissa Ford

AUTHOR BIOGRAPHY

Melissa Ford is a data analyst by day and a voracious reader by night. When she's not doing either of those things, she loves to perform long-form improv. Cupboard Maker Books is one of her favorite places on Earth, so she is especially thrilled to be part of this collection. This is Melissa's first published short story.

16

The Tenth Life of Squeekie the Bookstore Cat

Beth Ann Hargraves

Police Chief Jay Fry paced around the squad room. "So what do you think we should do, Graves?" As he paced he fiddled with a black pen.

Lieutenant Ann Graves sighed deeply. "I don't think we have a choice, really. I think we need to call in Squeekie."

Fry nodded grimly. "I hate to do it because it is so dangerous this time. I don't want the little guy to get hurt."

"Neither do I, but this is what he is trained to do." Graves opened her bottom desk drawer to retrieve her gun.

Fry drew in a deep breath just before he said "Okay. Let's go get him."

Cupboard Makers Books, Enola, Pennsylvania: 8:47 pm

Squeekie was sound asleep when he first heard the siren approaching from a distance. His ear perked and he opened one eye. Yawning he rolled onto his paws. Sticking his hind quarters up into the air he practiced his "downward dog."

Oh please, Squeekie thought, *cats have been doing that yoga position a heck of a lot longer than dogs!* Pushing himself upright he began his patrol of the store looking for anything even slightly amiss. Right as he moved through the romance section he heard a loud pounding on the door. *Who can it be this late? Certainly not a customer. The store has been closed for a while now.* He sauntered over to the door, flicking his tail and looked out the clear plastic of the new kitty door Michelle, the bookstore owner, installed. He saw two pairs of feet.

"Squeekie? Are you in there?" A man's rich baritone called out to him.

Ahh, thought Squeekie, *it was the Chief Jay Fry and his partner Lieutenant Ann Graves*. Squeekie jumped up onto a small table by the door and placed his paws on top of the deadlock. Using all of his weight he slid it open. Upon hearing the click he jumped down to the floor and pushed his head out of the flap in the door.

"Hey there Squeekie," Lieutenant Graves said softly just before she reached for the knob. Backing up, Squeekie sat at the door waiting for his friends to enter.

"Squeekie we really need your help tonight. We were just on 6th Street at the scene and we can't go through the front door of the warehouse without knowing what we would be running into. We can't see into the warehouse but you could enter through the roof vent and get us some video of the inside. The mayor's little girl, Molly, is being held captive and we are afraid that if the man who took her doesn't get his money before midnight he will kill her," Fry said with a frown.

Squeekie turned his gaze to Graves.

"So will you help?" she said bending to scratch behind his ear. Goodness he loves when she does that. Her hands are so gentle.

"There is some tuna in it for you buddy," Fry added hopefully.

Squeekie's ear perked up. He turned to let out several small meows calling George over to the door from his perch, sleeping high above the cash register.

"Oh what now, Squeekie," George said with some annoyance. "Don't you see I am trying to sleep here?!" George licked his paw and drew it to his left ear and rubbed all the way down his face.

"I need you to lock the door behind us," Squeekie replied through his teeth.

"Yeah, yeah. Have fun playing Keystone Kops." George swiftly dropped to the floor and watched Squeekie slide through the flap on the door.

Graves chuckled. "I guess he agrees and wants us to follow

him, Fry."

Fry nodded and opened the door leading her out. They saw Squeekie waiting patiently by the driver's side passenger door of their unmarked black SUV. Just as they began to move towards the car Graves heard the deadbolt click behind them.

These cats are scary smart, Graves thought. *Squeekie must have told the black cat to lock up for the night!*

Fry opened the rear door and retrieved something small and black from the backseat. Squeekie sat patiently as Fry slid on the vest that had been made for him and emblazoned with "Police" on each side. Velcroing it into place, Fry pinched Squeekie's velvety ear between his right forefinger and thumb and stroked it gently. "Okay bud, let's head over to the warehouse. We don't have a second to lose."

Squeekie could tell the situation is dire. Graves looked like she hadn't slept in days and Fry was a wrinkled mess under his own vest. It was as if neither of them had been home to shower, sleep or slip into fresh clothes in days. After Fry opened the door, Squeekie hopped up onto the back seat. Spinning three times he curled up into a little ball. Fry shut the door and got into the driver's seat as Grave walked briskly around the back of the SUV to join him inside.

O'Toole's Auto Parts Warehouse, Harrisburg, Pennsylvania: 9:26 pm

As Squeekie felt the car slowing he stretched again and sat looking out of the windows. He noticed there were police cars lining both sides of the street and portable light stations casting a terribly harsh glow. Despite the pervasive darkness of the late hour, Squeekie suspected a doctor could perform surgery under those lights. Fry parked the SUV just behind the police tape and opened Squeekie's door. Hopping down, Squeekie surveyed the scene. He had never seen so many police officers in one place!

"Hey Chief." Squeekie recognized the voice of Officer Gil Gonzales immediately. Brushing up against his legs he circled Gil and waited to be pet. Gonzales bent down and with a small smile stroked Squeekie's head saying hello. "Hey there Squeeks! We really need you tonight," Gonzales commented barely above a whisper.

No problem at all, Squeekie thought as he dipped his head to nod. Squeekie followed Fry, Gonzales and Graves over to the staging area weaving around officers strategically placed behind their car doors with guns drawn but pointed at no one. Once at the command tent, Squeekie jumped onto the table as some of the other officers snickered.

"Oh that damn cat. I can't believe they made him a vest!"

Squeekie shot them a look but did not bother to give them the time of his next furball. *Dogs have better manners than some humans and dogs lick their privates in public,* Squeekie thought.

"Okay Squeekie, would you hold still a moment so we can outfit you with a camera? We need to get a look at what is going on in that warehouse." Squeekie obliged and sat patiently as Graves deftly affixed the camera to the collar around his neck. Once secure, Squeekie turned his gaze to Fry.

"From the building plans we know there is a vent on the roof. If you could climb through that vent and give us a few good shots of the inside we could see where the girl is being held and if there is anyone else inside."

This certainly doesn't seem difficult; I only need to take a few minutes of video? With that, he jumped down from the portable table, crossed the street at a sprint and began his silent climb up the roof access staircase. The steps were worn and rusted after many years of neglect and each stung Squeekie's paws. As he was climbing higher he began to skip steps. He jumped over the ledge and onto the black tar rooftop. There was a man in a prone position with a gun pointed at the police below and his back to the vent. Staying low, Squeekie darted to the vent and flattened himself to the roof. While his vest covered most of his light coat his tail, feet and head are still exposed. Under the moonlight he knew he would practically shine.

Squeekie studied the vent. It was long and narrow and he was concerned that he would not fit with the added bulk of his vest and camera. Peering around the left side of the vent he confirmed that the man with the gun was still looking away and sent some video feed to the officers below documenting the man's location.

"Look at the screen," Graves said from below pointing to the left corner of the image, "there is a shooter on the roof but I can't make out his face."

Squeekie shimmied through the side of the vent with broken panels with some effort and a butt wiggle. The camera scraped along the metal vent flashing and Squeekie froze.

"Hey! Who's there?!" the man with the gun asked in a gruff whisper. Still lying on his stomach the gunman looks in the direction of the vent but Squeekie was wasting no time pushing though. He saw a maintenance catwalk about eight feet below him and knew the only option was to jump.

This will be easy. It's just like at Cupboard Maker Books.

The bookstore was equipped with all manners of shelves, ramps and catwalks for Squeekie and his friends to enjoy and use to prowl around. Dropping to the catwalk silently Squeekie took his first look at the floor.

Back at the command post Fry studied the live feed from Squeekie's camera. "It's a bit grainy, don't you think?"

"Well," Ann said sarcastically, "that is what happens when a police chief doesn't authorize any funding for new equipment."

"Ha ha, very funny," Fry said annoyed. "Feel free to do my thankless job anytime you'd like, princess."

From his position high on the catwalk Squeekie spotted the little girl, tied to a chair and staring at something sitting on the floor in front of her. *What is that thing?* Squeekie wondered. He walked slowly along the perimeter so he could get a better look at the front of the girl. There was something for sure sitting in front of her and it has a light that was blinking rhythmically on top of it. *NO,* Squeekie thought as he caught sight of all of the wires. *There is a bomb sitting at her feet!*

"Oh God," Graves said pointing at the screen. "Look at that. Do you think that is what it looks like it is?" She gasped. "We have to get her out of there!"

"But," Fry began, "how are we going to get around that guy with the rifle? He would pick us off one by one as we tried to get to the stairs. I don't think we can let on that we know he is there." Gonzales nodded and contributed his two cents.

"I agree with the Chief. It would be a bloodbath."

"Do you think it is the kidnapper or an accomplice? I can't tell from the video feed," Graves said with some panic in her voice.

Looking frantically for any other humans Squeekie was satisfied the girl was alone in the room. He found some crates stacked near the wall of the warehouse and began his descent to the floor. The floor was cold, filthy and the paint was peeling in places. He padded swiftly to the girl at a wide angle so that she could see him coming and wouldn't scream. Her wrists and ankles are bound to the metal chair by rope, and each was bleeding and bruised. It was clear she put up a struggle and it was clearer she had been crying for quite some time.

"Oh," she gasped quietly. She studied Squeekie before saying "a police *cat?* Are there policemen outside?!" Squeekie flicked his tail and rubbed up against her legs. Outside Fry and Graves were glued to the monitor.

"Come on, Squeeks! Get a shot of everything!" Fry said exasperated.

As if on cue, Squeekie circled the girl slowly and provided footage, albeit in wide angle video. *It is nearly impossible to judge distance or proximity in wide angle video*! Squeekie thought. He stopped moving the camera after a while and settled it on the bomb.

"Oh," Graves breathed staring intently at the monitor. "That's definitely a bomb, isn't it?"

Squeekie closed in on the small bomb taking care to show all sides. He knew, with the man on the roof, that no one with opposable thumbs would be coming in the front door to help the little girl until the man was neutralized. Squeekie did the only thing he could think of to do to help; he began chewing his way through her restraints.

O'Toole's Auto Parts Warehouse: 10:24 pm

Squeekie's mouth ached and his gums were bleeding but he

knew he had to persist until she was free. From outside Fry and Graves watched the feed, somewhat confused about what they were seeing.

"What is he looking at? Can you make out what it is?" Fry asked no one in particular.

"He is awfully close to something, that's for sure," Graves replied.

Squeekie finally managed to chew through the last of the tough rope restraints and the girl shook free and stood. Brushing up against her legs he started to purr in an effort to put the little human at ease. She was scared enough without having to stare down at a housecat with blood in the fur by his mouth like *Cujo*. The acidic, copper taste of blood filled Squeekie's mouth and he was glad he ate hours ago because his appetite vanished faster than a dog that shredded a full roll of toilet paper. Once he had backed away from the girl his friends outside got a better picture of what was going on inside.

"There's Molly," Graves whispered to Fry.

"Yes, and there is rope on the floor. Wait," Fry paused just a moment before finishing his thought, "did the cat chew through her restraints!?"

Squeekie ran around the warehouse looking for any way out that would be big enough for the child to escape through. He was coming up with nothing. *There must be some way,* he thought. The doors were locked from the inside with giant chains and locks, probably the only two things in the entire warehouse that weren't covered in rust. There weren't any windows. In some places crates full of auto parts, presumably, were stacked floor to ceiling. He tried to communicate with by making eye contact with the five year old and motioned left and right with his tail.

"Kitty...help me. I am scared," she said softly, tears staining her cheeks.

I know, kiddo, we have to find a way out. You must have come in the front door but it is locked now.

"I am not sure how we came in. I was really sleepy and a big man carried me."

Squeekie stopped dead. *She can hear me?*

"Of course I can hear you, silly. You are talking to me, aren't you?" Molly smiled slightly and began twisting a lock of her blonde hair in between her fingers.

Start to look around those boxes. Maybe there is a grate or something I can push out. There are a lot of police officers outside that will take you to your family. Squeekie crossed the room away from her and began to weave in and around all of the boxes in his path. Finally Molly piped up from across the warehouse.

"There is something over here beside this big box." Squeekie sprinted towards her to see that there was a large grate. When he pressed his ears up against it he heard the sounds of police radios and talking from outside.

Perfect! Great job, Molly. Squeekie was dismayed when he saw the rusted vent was screwed into place. There was no way he was going to get those screws loosened. There was really only one other option at this point. He would have to run headlong into the grate, slam into it with his body and hope he could damage it enough that the little girl could squeeze through one side.

From outside Fry and Graves saw the grate on the video feed. "Is that the north side of the building?" He studied the frame more closely.

Graves began to run towards the warehouse, ignoring warnings from her fellow officers, and as a reward she heard a bullet whiz by her left side. Pressing herself along the brick face of the building she made her way across the front and around to the north side. She found the grate and knelt, still pressed as tightly as possible to the building. Officers from the street responded with a barrage of shots and the man on the roof took cover. Graves looked up. With the overhang of the building's roof she would be protected from any shots by the suspect.

Inside Squeekie prepared for the pain associated with running headlong into something. Closing his eyes briefly he then met the worried gaze of the small child. Squeekie purred. *I'll be okay, my dear. You just close your eyes tight and don't open them until I tell you to.* Molly nodded and closed her eyes. On cue, Squeekie ran as fast as he could at the grate and slammed his body into it, hard. The grate dented and pulled away from one side. Squeekie was a bit stunned and staggered away towards Molly.

Outside Graves heard the thud and shifting her weight onto her butt she began kicking the grate with both feet. It gave easily, probably due to the copious amounts of rust that seemed to paralyze this old warehouse. Rolling on her stomach she pulled the flashlight from her jacket pocket and illuminated the inside of the duct. Much to her surprise she saw two pairs of eyes staring back at her.

"Hi Molly, my name is Lieutenant Ann Graves. I see you met Squeekie, our police cat. Do you think you can crawl towards me?"

"Yes, but I think Squeekie is hurt, bad. He's bleeding." Squeekie flicked his tail weakly at Molly and tried his best to purr.

"I will take Squeekie to a doctor but you have to crawl to me first." Molly nodded and got onto her hands and knees and slowly made her way towards Graves.

"I think there are spiders in here! I hate spiders!" Molly whimpered.

"Nothing will hurt you. You're doing great. Keep coming towards me." From the street, Fry was watching on the monitor when suddenly the picture turned sideways.

It was Fry's turn to sprint to the building, carefully avoiding any crossfire in the firefight. When he arrived at Graves he was short of breath and feared for Squeekie. "Graves, I think Squeekie is hurt in there. Do you think I can fit through the grate?"

Just then Molly crawled out, covered in spider webs, and crying.

"They are crawling on me! Get them OFF!"

Fry drew Molly into his chest and began brushing the webs away from her face and neck and finally out of her hair.

"No Fry, I don't think you can fit," she paused, "...but I can." Placing the flashlight between her teeth Graves moved as quickly as she could through the duct. When she reached the other side she pushed hard on the bent vent. She saw Squeekie slumped onto his side, breathing very shallowly, with blood coming from his mouth.

"Oh God!" Graves shouted. "Come on Squeeks! Stay with me." Leaving his side momentarily she looked at the timing device on the bomb. It was a cell phone. One call could explode the building sky high! Tying her jacket into a cocoon she gently placed Squeekie inside and began to crawl once again through the duct, scraping her hands and tearing the knees of her pants.

Once Fry saw Graves nearly at the end of the tunnel he radioed the command post to push the officers back from the building. With Molly safe in his arms and Squeekie safe in Grave's jacket they darted to the ambulances down the block from the scene, which now sounded like the last gunfight at the O.K. Corral.

The EMTs checked over both Molly and Squeekie and pronounced them in good health, albeit a bit banged up. Fry returned to the center of the scene, grabbed his bullhorn and shouted up at the suspect on the roof.

"This is Chief Jay Fry. We have you surrounded. It's over Spender! Surrender now and we won't shoot you." Spender peered over the wall slightly and shouted back.

"Come even one inch towards me and I will blow the building and the little girl away."

Fry chuckled into the bullhorn.

"What's so funny, pig?" Spender shouted.

"We have the girl. Took her right out from under your nose. Go ahead, blow the building. Save the city the trouble. It has been slated for demolition anyway. Come down peacefully or you'll burn up in the blast too."

Spender didn't seem to think about his options very long.

"If I go, I'm taking all of you with me." Graves, having returned to Fry's side, saw him reach for something in his pocket.

"He's got a cell phone!" She screamed. "EVERYONE TAKE COVER!"

With one loud pop Spender tumbled right over the ledge and landed, hard, on the gravel in front of the warehouse. Grave's head whipped around and she saw Gonzales holding a rifle.

Gun drawn, Fry cautiously approached the man, crouched beside him and placed two fingers on the artery in his neck. Fry shook his head and looked at Graves as if to say "No pulse."

It wouldn't be until the autopsy if the ME would be able to determine if the gunshot wound or the fall killed Spencer, but none of officers seemed to care, in Squeekie's opinion, as he watched from the back of the ambulance.

Mystery Cupboard Books, Enola, Pennsylvania: Two Weeks Later

The door of the book shop sprang open and Fry and Graves walked in looking for Squeekie. On cue Squeekie limped over to them and began purring furiously.

"Hey there, sport. Good to see you back on your feet." Squeekie flipped his tail motioning for the Lieutenant and Chief to follow. Next to his bed were dozens of get well cards, mouse toys and even a "bouquet" of catnip.

"Looks like you have a lot of admirers," Graves commented, "and with good reason. You did a fantastic job! Well above and beyond a feline's call of duty. Little Molly will be having a sixth birthday this week all because of you."

I think it was a bit of a team effort, don't you? Where would I be if you didn't come into the warehouse, one which contained a bomb I might add, to save me? All Graves heard was a series of meows.

Fry chuckled. "I think he is trying to tell you something, Graves."

"Oh, and before we forget, some of us at the station got together to give this to you." Graves placed a large shopping bag filled with cans of fine Canadian tuna in front of Squeekie. Squeekie's eyes widened and he purred in appreciation.

Not a bad way to spend my tenth life, he thought.

Beth Ann Hargraves

AUTHOR BIOGRAPHY

Beth Ann was born and raised in Pennsylvania and now resides in Camp Hill. She received her bachelor's degree in history and political science from Washington College, her Master's degree from West Chester University of Pennsylvania and a certificate in paralegal studies from Harrisburg Area Community College. She enjoys running, watching movies and spending time with her family and friends. Beth Ann abhors anything mint flavored and getting caught in the rain.

17

The Way of the Beloved Kitty

Heidi Hormel

I am the Double Fanged Terror, slayer of stinkbugs and killer of Mousey-Mouse. I rule my domain with razor teeth and Claws of Steel. Watch me fly through the air like a dragon ninja.

I will amuse myself with my musings and my acrobatics.

"Cat," My Human says as I test my claws on the Cat Who Gets All the Laps. She will know that this reclining throne is mine. *Scratch, scratch.* "Stop it," says My Human again. I glance with disdain, shaking my fluffy brown and cream fur into order. I am the Double Fanged Terror.

Then the liquid of death hits my shoulder. I must run from the water, the bringer of feline humiliation. I find a safe space under the fortress of human food and lick my water wounds. It tastes better than it feels.

I peer from beneath the fortress's veil, watching for My Human and the She Who Gets All the Laps. I will nap to reserve my strength.

"Richard," My Human says, but I keep my eyes closed. If I cannot see her, she cannot see me. "Ricky." She's getting closer. Then hands around me. I struggle for a moment.

These meetings often end in Delightful Treats. I calm myself and watch over her shoulder. It's like being on top of the humming food box. I can watch everything around me. There is Mousey-Mouse. I must remember to come back and destroy him with my Blue Glare of Annihilation, even though he lacks the squeaks I love to hear as I vanquish my foes.

"Here he is," My Human says. "I know all of his hiding places."

"Mew, mew, mew," I yell my voice hoarse with embarrassing fear. It is MAL-OR-EE. The most terrifying Human in my domain. I dig in my claws so I can leap to safety. My Human screams. The MAL-OR-EE makes a grab. I show my double fang — *No.* She touches me and I strike out with my front claw and I'm free. I race up the stairway to safety. I find the space that My Human and She Who Gets All the Laps don't fit.

Must slow my breathing. I got away. I am safe. I am the Double Fanged Terror. I do not ever need to be the Beloved Kitty, like She Who Gets All the Laps.

"Mew. Mew," I say. *Wait. What?* I'm picked up disturbing my Sleep of Restoration and put into the Box of Torture. It moves. I put out my Claws of Steel to keep from falling, then the noise of a machine and the sway. I hate the sway. It always ends in the Place of Bad Smells, where they poke me in places no cat should ever be poked. But the sway is different. It is longer. *Where are we going?* "Roar?" I try to get My Human's attention. She must stop. "Grr," I say for the first time ever. She must understand I am serious about the stopping. But she doesn't listen.

So long later that I cannot count the number of naps it would take, the swaying stops. I am still in the Box of Torture, but now we are outside, then we are in a new house that is not a house. I smell and hear other felines. It is not She Who Gets All of the Laps. Another one who smells— "Meowar."

The sound is familiar. Is it a new enemy? Or … I bow down as he approaches the Box of Torture. It is the legend — Obi-Squeekie-wan. I lived with him many bowls of Crunchy Delights ago. Why have I been brought here again?

"I'm hoping you can help me with Richard. He runs from visitors and poor Mallory can't get near him," says My Human

Was the MAL-OR-EE here? Must hide. There is no place in the Box of Torture. I move, it sways.

"Stop that," says My Human. Finally the box is on solid ground.

"I'm not sure how we can help?" says another Human.

The Way of the Beloved Kitty

"Actually, I thought maybe Squeekie could show him how to get along with people? You know, like Richard could be his intern or something? Squeekie is a Siamese, too, even though he doesn't have long hair like Ricky, and he is so good with everybody including little kids."

"I don't know. We've haven't done anything like that before. What do you think, Squeekie?"

"Maowar," answers Obi-Squeekie-wan. He is not pleased. He says that I cannot learn anything.

"Mew," I answer because I can learn. I am the Double Fanged Terror.

"Rrr." Obi-Squeekie-wan laughs at me.

My Human says, "I'm desperate. If he doesn't act better around Mallory, I may have to find him a new place. We've tried everything. Maybe he's just not happy at my house?"

What is My Human saying? That she'll leave me here? "Mew?" I ask. She doesn't answer, but Obi-Squeekie-wan does with a bump against the Box of Torture.

"Mewl?" he asks. *Are you ready to learn now? I tried to instruct you many Crunchy Delights ago, but you would not listen.*

"Mow." *I am ready and willing. I do not want to leave My Human.*

"OK," says the other Human.

"Great. I've brought food and his special toys." My Human's voice gets closer. "Ricky, I don't want to leave you here but you must learn. I'll bring you home as soon as I can because I know Mallory already misses you."

I look through the slots. *Is the MAL-OR-EE here?*

Obi-Squeekie-wan makes a low sound and bumps the Box of Torture again. He says that *the MAL-OR-EE is another Human, and I must learn that the short humans are even more important than the tall ones.*

No way. They do not bring the Crunchy Delights and they **grab**.

Here is your first lesson, Richard: Stop and they will not grab.

Before I can answer, the door on the Box of Torture is opened, and I am out like the wind of the night, past Obi-Squeekie-wan and off to find a Cave of Security.

"Ricky," My Human calls, but I must ignore her. No matter what Obi-Squeekie-wan says I cannot stay if the MAL-OR-EE is near.

I am hungry but there is the smell of other felines and Obi-Squeekie-wan says I may not have any Crunchy Delights until I can say hello to each one. I creep along the floor. I know she is near. Obi-Squeekie-wan says her name is Annika. She is like me, fluffy haired and puffy tailed, but her nose is short, not noble like mine. I see her. She stares at me. I look away as I've been taught by Obi-Squeekie-wan. Annika makes a low growl like She Who Gets All the Laps. I go lower to the floor so she cannot see me. Then Obi-Squeekie-wan says, *You must approach her or you will never become a Beloved Kitty.*

You can show me the way of the Beloved Kitty?

Of course, he answers, his light blue eyes sparkling.

I look up and to the side. Annika sits and watches me. I am brave. I am the Double Fanged Terror. I race to her. She swats me with a paw and it rings through my brain.

"Meow," says Obi-Squeekie-wan, telling me that I have approached Annika in every way that is wrong. In a low purr, he explains that I must approach her with respect.

"Mew," I say. *I am the Double Fanged Terror and she should respect me first.*

Obi-Squeekie-wan tells me he doesn't care. *If I want to be a Beloved Kitty that means respecting other felines and making friends, not enemies or minions.*

"Me-rowr," Obi-Squeekie-wan says. He and I will need to spend much time together at the Home of Books and Shelves until I understand exactly how to be a cat, the first step in becoming a Beloved Kitty.

So begins my training in humiliation and respect. I must sleep with the kittens, even though I am a superior full-grown fluffy cat. I growl and swat the kittens who try to touch my tail. Obi-Squeekie-wan and Annika quickly come and discipline me.

I eventually learn to play without biting or taunting. Next, I

The Way of the Beloved Kitty

learn to visit with Annika and she teaches me to groom fluffy fur properly and to stare without staring at the other felines.

When Obi-Squeekie-wan says that I am now past the first step in the Way of the Beloved Kitty. I purr with joy.

Many meals of Crunchy Delights later, I have passed the Stillness of Clipping, when the human takes silver to my nails. Then the pleasure-pain of the brush is endured. I could be one step closer to Beloved Kitty after today, Obi-Squeekie-wan says. It will be my greatest challenge so far. *The Human Carry, Pet, and Grab must be accepted and enjoyed.*

"Raowr," Obi-Squeekie-wan says, *Today there will be more humans than I have ever seen at the Home of Books and Shelves. My job will be to allow humans – no matter their size -- to touch me without running away.*

The other felines look down on me from the Cloud Walks. Annika lays on the counter and sniffs as she says I am like her and will never be a Beloved Kitty. It is the curse of the Fluffy Cat. *We turn into wild animals at the touch of new humans.* Obi-Squeekie-wan tells her that she is wrong. He says Annika is not wild but a Scaredy Cat.

We all wait for the fight. Annika sniffs again and saunters away with a disdainful wave of her tail.

I watch Annika's fluffy tail and imagine the hands of strange humans touching and grasping me. Maybe I am a Cursed Fluffy Cat. My whiskers twitch. I do not want to do this, but I do want to be a Beloved Kitty.

I walk to Obi-Squeekie-wan and ask if there isn't another test. *I can jump from the highest Cloud Walk to the counter.* He says that it must be the strange humans. He stares at me and doesn't let me look away.

"Meow," he says because my stare shows bravery, certainly enough to face the strange humans. When I become a Beloved Kitty, Obi-Squeekie-wan says I will get extra Delightful Treats and the best thing ever, which I will only know after I become a Beloved Kitty. Do I want to miss that?

No. I am the Double Fanged Terror. I fear nothing, not even Strange Humans and their grasping hands.

I follow Obi-Squeekie-wan to the counter. There is a group of Small Humans. The worst kind. The kind that must be avoided.

"Mewl," says Obi-Squeekie-wan pushing me forward to my next test in the Way of the Beloved Kitty. *Stand up tall,* he tells me.

I try so hard to walk tall, not crouch so the small humans don't see me. I hear a jeer from Annika who reminds me I am a Cursed Fluffy Cat. But that's not what I want. I want to be a Beloved Kitty. I force my legs to un-crouch. Obi-Squeekie-wan points out to my ears. They are flat to my head. *That is not the proper position.*

"Look, Mommy," says a Small Human. "Fuffy kitty."

Steady, purrs my mentor. *Watch me.*

I stand in horror as I see Obi-Squeekie-wan go right up to the Small Human and get patted on the head then pulled into a squeezing hug. This is worse than anything I've ever seen. Ever. How can my mentor expect me to do that? How does he do that?

"Preddy kitty," says the Small Human and releases my mentor, who walks to another human for a pet and ... a Delightful Treat.

A Delightful Treat? That may be worth a grab by the Small Human. I move forward. The Small Human squeals. My ears lay down and Obi-Squeekie-wan growls so no one else hears except me and Annika. She sneers and purrs a chuckle.

I will be a Beloved Kitty. I am not afraid like Annika.

"Look, Mommy, another kitty" says the Small Human loud enough to break my ears. Obi-Squeekie-wan is watching.

I move closer and closer to the Small Human watching the hands with the graspy fingers. *I can do this. I am the Double Fanged Terror.*

"Meow," says Obi-Squeekie-wan, reminding me I must go closer or I will never be a Beloved Kitty.

I slip one paw nearer. I allow my tail to go straight up and put my ears into the happy pose. The Small Human squeals again. My ears don't move. I place my paw closer, Claws of Steel sheathed.

The Small Human lunges forward, hand out and her fingers pat hard on my head. My eyes close, but I don't move.

"Careful, honey," says a Large Human.

The Way of the Beloved Kitty

"Maowr," says Obi-Squeekie-wan. *Don't move. Don't scratch. Don't growl.*

I nearly lose my nerve when the face of the Small Human comes closer, followed by a smooch on the top of my head.

"Grr," says Annika and races away. She is disappointed I have not failed this hardest test.

The Small Human gives me one more pat and moves away.

"Blurp," I say. *I have passed the test.*

Obi-Squeekie-wan says, *You have more tests, but you have done well.*

I strut through the Home of Books and Shelves. I allow one more human to touch me without running and without moving my ears. This is easy.

Today is the final, final test. If I pass it, I will become a Beloved Kitty (and get special Crunchy Delights). I walk around the Home of Books and Shelves, my tail waving and my ears in happy pose. The other felines on their way to Beloved Kitty look at me in awe.

Annika flattens her ears and laughs at me. "K-hiss," she says. *Fluffy Cats are cursed.*

I'm ready to bump her nose when Obi-Squeekie-wan calls me. *It is time.*

I saunter to the front of the store to stand with Obi-Squeekie-wan. He reminds me, *You cannot run away. You cannot growl. You cannot scratch. And, most importantly, you cannot bite.*

"Mcowr," I say with confidence. *I've got this. I have passed all the other tests. I will pass this one. I am the Double Fanged Terror.*

"Mew," says Obi-Squeekie-wan. *Don't be so sure. This is not like the others.*

My mentor stares at me. I have learned to look down and not challenge him.

"Blerp?" I ask, wondering when the test will start. Obi-Squeekie-wan eyes glance to the door. My test is here.

I sit as Obi-Squeekie-wan does, my eyes closed enough to look like I'm snoozing, calm with my ears in sleepy pose. I wait.

"Richard," My Human says. My eyes pop open.

"Mew," Obi-Squeekie-wan says quietly. *This is not the test.*

Still, I stand and put my tail in the air and ears in happy pose. My Human gives me pets and pats. They all feel good, not like they used to.

"Ricky," the MAL-OR-EE says.

I freeze. A protest growls through me.

"Maowr," says Obi-Squeekie-wan. *No growling.*

But this is the MAL-OR-EE. He does not understand. I must get away. I cannot—

"Richard, we're here to take you home. You're ready now," My Human says as she and the MAL-OR-EE swarm around me.

I can't breathe. I must get away. I climb the MAL-OR-EE with my claws of steel. Must get to the Cloud Walks. I leap. I yowl louder than the MAL-OR-EE.

Annika chuckles.

I pant on the walkway. Obi-Squeekie-wan shakes his head in disgust. My Human glares at me. The MAL-OR-EE cries.

I run low to the walkway and find a dark corner to hide. My breathing slows. How did I ever think I could become a Beloved Kitty. Annika was right. I am a Cursed Fluffy Cat.

I hear the other felines munching on Delightful Treats. I am not hungry. I cannot show my disgraced self.

"Richard," says My Human. "Come here kitty. Come on kitty." There is a long pause. I can only hear the crunching. "Maybe we'll have to leave him here if he isn't any better with Mallory."

Leave me. No. But I have failed. I am not a Beloved Kitty. I crouch further into my dark hole.

"He doesn't mean it," says the MAL-OR-EE. "Maybe Squeekie just needs more time to teach him manners. Please. Can't we wait. I love him so much."

Love me? The MAL-OR-EE loves me? I never imagined that. She always grabbed me, chased me. What had Obi-Squeekie-wan said? *Stop. Wait. And, then, no grab. You teach them by not moving.* Was that true? Yes. It had worked with the even smaller humans.

I creep from my dark hole. "Blu-urp," I say. *Wait.* I race along

The Way of the Beloved Kitty

the Cloud Walk. "Blu-urp."

"Meoawr," says Obi-Squeekie-wan. *Hurry.*

I scamper along the planks and leap to the floor, running faster and faster. There they are. By the clear doors. "Mewl," I say. *Don't leave.* The MAL-OR-EE turns. I hesitate. She will grab me and then— She'll love me. That's why she grabs me.

"Mew," says Obi-Squeekie-wan. *Now, you understand.*

I stop in front of the MAL-OR-EE. "Mewlor," I say. *Don't leave without me.*

"Ricky," she says. Her grasping hands reach out. I do not move. I am as still and calm as Obi-Squeekie-wan. Her hand does not grab. It pets. My Human stands behind her now, smiling at me.

"Oh, what a good boy," she says. "He likes you."

I wouldn't go that far, but —

"Maowr," says Obi-Squeekie-wan, reminding me that I am nearly a beloved kitty. I must not move. I must accept the pats, pets, hugs, and kisses from the MAL-OR-EE. My ultimate test.

"Ricky," the MAL-OR-EE says and grasps me in a big hug.

I do not move, then the squeeze feels good on my sides. I bump my head against her chin to let her know that I understand she loves me and I love her.

"Mewlr," says Obi-Squeekie-wan. *You are a Beloved Kitty.* The other felines cheer. Annika sniffs with disdain.

As I leave, held in the arms of the MAL-OR-EE, I say, "Mewl," to Annika. *One day you will be brave enough to be a Beloved Kitty.*

"Grrrl," she answers. *Never.*

"Blerp," I say just before the doors close. *You can teach an old cat new tricks.*

Heidi Hormel

AUTHOR BIOGRAPHY

A former innkeeper and radio talk show host, **Heidi Hormel** has always been a writer. She spent years as a small-town newspaper reporter and as a PR flunky before settling happily into penning romances with a wink and a wiggle.

While living in the Snack Food Capital of the World, Heidi has trotted around the globe from forays into Death Valley to stops at Loch Ness in Scotland.

She has published five books in the Angel Crossing, Arizona series with Harlequin Western Romance. To sign up for her newsletter or to read more about her books, visit www.HeidiHormel.net or follow her on Facebook and Twitter.

18

Tiny, Mighty Heroes

Teddy Maurer

A streak of tan fur flashed by the Romance section, zoomed down the Fantasy aisle and into the Non-Fiction room of the Cupboard Maker Books store. There, Squeekie skidded to a stop in front of a small hole in the corner. Beneath the baseboard, a tiny bit of gray stuck out of the shadow. His eyes narrowed as he poised for a pounce.

"I've got you now, Robena!"

"No you ain't, Squeek. I's too fast for you. You's gettin' old an' fat."

"Oh yeah? You skinny excuse for a mouse, you're going to be missing a tail in a minute."

"Says you, you's cross-eyed, fish breathed dog bait."

Squeekie gathered his weight and with a quick wiggle to gauge his distance, sprang forward like a spark of electricity. Robena skittered deeper into the opening to avoid his outreached claws.

"Ha ha. Missed me. Betters luck nex'ed time, ol friend."

"Bah, you little pain in the butt. Tomorrow is another day."

"Goods night Squeek. Sleeps well. I's here fer talkin' if yous gets bored."

"Yeah, yeah, yeah. Remember, no chewing on the books and no poo pellets left laying around the store. Got it?"

"Whys yous keeps remindin' me? I's keeps my parts of da deal. Yous lets me stays here an I's promises to behave."

"How many babies do you have back there anyway? I can

smell at least four. Have you told them about the rules?"

"They's only days old, Squeek. They's eyes ain't open yet. And they's six by da way."

"They better not break the rules when they start to wander around on their own. They can't stay here either. They must move on. This is a book store, not a mouse motel."

"Theys'll behave. Goods nights Squeek."

Squeekie flicked his tail and withdrew his paw from the tunnel.

"See that they do. Good-night, Robena."

He sauntered out of the room and jumped onto the carpeted cat tower. He moved silently along its path spanning the aisles nearly nine feet above the floor.

"Good night Poppy. Good night Pepe. Good night Miss Cassie. Good night Tommy."

"Good night Squeekie," the cats meowed in unison.

Satisfied that everyone was safely accounted for, Squeekie settled down in his favorite spot above the cash register. From there he had a bird's eye view of his domain. He licked his paw, wiped it across his ear, over his eye and down his nose – over and over again. He changed paws and did the same on the other side of his head. Satisfied with his spotless face, he lifted a back leg, pointed his toes skyward and cleaned his belly fur.

"I've liked her ever since I found her with a broken leg but that mouse is going be the death of me yet." He paused his preening to say to himself. "I must be getting soft in the head."

The bookstore was still, and those who called it home settled down for the night. Headlights from the occasional car whooshing by streaked across the aisles of books, in an arc around the room, revealing the cats perched throughout the store. The tick-tock rhythm of the clock behind the counter soothed Squeekie. He purred with satisfaction at the orderly state of his world and drifted off to sleep.

The serenity was shattered by a deafening boom, like a cannon shot. The sky lit up bright blue and it sparkled with small red glitter falling downward.

Squeekie's every hair stood on end as he sprang from his

peaceful slumber and landed harshly on his stiff legs. He searched the room for a source of the commotion.

"What was that, Squeekie?"

"I don't know, Cassie. It sounded like a full book shelf fell over!"

"No, Squeekie, it came from outside and there was a big flash of blue light that lit up the sky."

"Flash of light... "

Squeekie looked around the room and there, on the counter, the calendar page caught his eye.

"Ah, Fourth of July. Independence Day! That explains it, Miss Cassie. Humans celebrate this day with a noisy display of fireworks."

Again the night was marked by a boom and a burst of light.

"Ugh, the smell of those things is awful. How long will this go on?"

"Until it's over, Pepe. I hope it's soon."

"Squeek, Squeek! They's people in da parkin' lot. I's wents outside to see whats'll dat noise was. Squeek, they's using matches an' they's bombs goin' ways up into da air an' they's makin' dem noises."

"Robena. Robena! Calm down. It's July 4th. Humans celebrate today this way."

"But Squeek, they's put fire on da roof."

"Fire on our roof?"

"Yes, I seed it wit my own eyes!"

Squeekie ran to the front door and with his nose pressed against the glass, next to the "Don't Let the Cats Out" sign, he watched several young men throw something into the trunk of a car. They quickly jumped into the car and as they sped out of the parking lot, gravel flew from beneath the spinning wheels.

"Oh no, they're leaving," Squeekie said. "They're not calling the police. We've got to do something before the bookstore burns down."

"What can we do?" Poppy asked.

"Let me think," Squeekie said.

"Squeek, they's higher flames on da roof. My babies..."

"Robena, calm down. We're going to save this store."

Robena ran in circles around Squeekie's legs. The other cats lined up at the front door, peering into the empty parking lot.

"Squeek, I's gonna gets help from da mice next door. We's can pulls dat hose ups to da roof to puts out dat fire."

"That's a great idea, Robena. Hurry! While you're doing that, I'm going to try to call for help. I've seen Michelle use that phone a million times."

Robena scurried around the corner and into the crack in the baseboard. Squeekie watched her run across the parking lot and into the garage next door, then he jumped onto the counter. He sat in front of the phone and deftly knocked the handset away from the base. The dial tone buzz, echoed in the quiet room.

"I have to push these buttons but which ones."

He took a chance by pushing the most prominent button he saw, one with a red sticker on it and waited.

"9-1-1. What is the emergency?"

Cassie, Pepe, Poppy and Tommy cheered.

"You pushed the right button!"

Squeekie motioned them to be quiet.

"Our roof is on fire. We need help."

"Hello" Is anyone there?" the 9-1-1 operator questioned.

"I'm Squeekie. We need firemen to put out the fire on our bookstore roof. Hurry, please!"

"Hello?"

"Our store is on fire! Please send help!"

"Joe, I've got a call here with nothing but a bunch of cats meowing. Yes, the line is still open but all I hear is cats. No, it's quiet otherwise. Do you think it's cats being cats or should we send the police?"

There was a pause.

"Got it. Caller ID is (717) 732-7288. Umm, Cupboard Maker Books, 157 N Enola Rd, Enola. Send the police, Joe, and try to reach Michelle Haring, the owner. Her home phone number is listed on the commercial property report. I'll keep this connection open until I hear the police."

Tiny, Mighty Heroes

By now, the mice crew had organized. They had tied one end of a rope to a lightweight expandable hose, hooked up to the outside faucet and took the other end over a tree limb. The group pulled the free end of the rope in unison and slowly stretched the hose to its full length. It hung above the one story building.

"Stops friends. Its is up as fars as its'll go. Ties dat end of da rope to somethin' so its'll don't falls down an' then wes'll works together to turns on da water. Den, wes'll climb up dat tree and out theys limb to aim at dat fire. Gots it?"

"Got it Robena!"

The mice proceeded to tie the loose end of the rope around a huge flower pot. They struggled to turn the faucet on, then, in a single row, they climbed up the tree. The hose was shooting a stream of water away from the fire and it was swinging wildly.

"Sparkie, you's da biggest. Gits out on dat hose and wes'll follow you so's its'll stop swingin'."

Gripping the rope, Sparkie followed it to the end of the hose and wrapped himself around it. The swinging motion slowed allowing the other mice to follow his lead. By changing their positions, and the balance on the hose, they aimed the water flow toward the fire. The water sizzled and danced across the shingles. The smoke billowed as the flames shrank.

"It's is workin'. Dis fire, its'll soon be out."

"Sees da car? They's the police an' its means help is on da way."

As the police car pulled into the bookstore parking lot with lights flashing and siren blaring, the mice cheered with glee.

The patrolmen, at the sight of smoke and flames, immediately contacted dispatch to alert the fire company. Before getting out of the patrol car, officers Jamal and Sam leaned closer to the windshield and looked at the hose hanging from the tree.

"Jamal, look up there," Sam said. "Do you see what I see?"

"What in the world is that rigged up in the tree?"

"Whatever it is, it's keeping the flames to a minimum. Dispatch, we are witnessing something odd."

"Dispatch here. What do you mean odd?"

"We're here at Cupboard Maker Books and the roof is on fire."

"Yes. Besides tragic, what's odd about that?"

"That's not what's strange. There's a hose tied to a tree branch, shooting water onto the fire. That's the odd thing."

"Is anyone there with this hose?"

"Not that we see. What's the ETA on the fire crew?"

"Stand-by while I check."

"Hey, Sam. Grab the flashlight," Jamal said. "Let's get a closer look at that set-up."

Sirens echoed in the distance, blared louder as the firetruck traveled toward the bookstore and stopped abruptly after the truck slid to a stop in the parking lot.

"Dispatch to car 22. Sam, ETA..."

"Never mind, dispatch, they're here. Thanks."

Amid the flashing lights, revving engine of the truck, and the night air filled with smoke, the firemen rushed toward the fire with ladders and limp hoses over their shoulders. They quickly extended a ladder and propped it up against the eaves of the bookstore.

"Jumping Jack Rabbits! Did you see that Dave?"

"What the... was that mice running from the hose hanging in the tree?"

"Sure looked like mice to me, Mac," Dave said. "A bunch of 'em too! They've got a serious infestation here. Hey, Mike, open the hydrant and turn off that little garden hose, will ya?"

The fire hose stiffened as it filled and it shot a thick stream of water onto the burning roof. Within a matter of minutes, the small fire was extinguished. Thankfully, while the wooden roof was charred, the fire was primarily limited to the shingles and several layers of tar paper.

The store owner, Michelle, had arrived and provided a key to the store so the firemen could check for hot spots inside the building.

"All clear, ma'am. There is a small amount of water damage but you were lucky someone kept the fire at bay with the garden hose. I have to tell ya, lady, you need to get a pest control

Tiny, Mighty Heroes

company in here. The rodents were scurrying everywhere to escape the fire."

"Mice? In here? Mister, I have rescue cats living inside the store. I find it hard to believe I have a rodent problem."

"All I'm telling you is what we saw when we started up the ladder."

"Yeah, George. I saw 'em too," Jamal said. "They were hanging on the garden hose. I'm bettin' they were getting toasty there too, hangin' over the flames like that."

"Mice hanging on the hose? Yeah right," Michelle said, rolling her eyes. "I think all the smoke affected your vision. Maybe you two should take a little oxygen? There is a tank of it on the truck - right?"

Mac chuckled. "Ma'am, we don't need oxygen. Thanks to whoever was using that garden hose before we got here, this fire was kept small. Another unique thing about this call – dispatch said it was called in by cats."

"Cats?" Michelle smiled sheepishly. Right then she knew who had made the call to the fire company. The phone was off the hook when she came into the store which was odd but it all made sense now. She turned from the firemen, walked toward the front door and swung it open.

"Thanks for getting here so quickly to put out the fire. I'll make an additional donation to your station."

"It's our job, ma'am but you're welcome." After walking through the door, Mac faced Michelle. "The chief will be in touch with you in the morning," he said. "The investigators will work with you to determine what caused the fire."

Before she left the store for the night, Michelle checked the litter boxes and made sure there was plenty of food and fresh water for her store cats. She scratched each of them behind the ears and told them what good kitties they were. Squeekie got special attention.

"I know it was you. You made the call, didn't you? I don't know how the mice are involved and I'm not sure I want to know but thank-you, Squeekie. You're the best cat ever!"

Remnants of the firecrackers were found in the parking lot

and because the flash-point of the fire was nowhere near anything mechanical that would cause a fire, it was ruled as vandalism. While it was doubtful the perpetrators would ever be found, Michelle felt better knowing there was nothing electrically wrong with the building. She and her employees labored for weeks to return the store to its usual working order. On the night before the store was ready to reopen, she set up a little party area on the floor of the back room. Complete with a tablecloth, party hats, plates and confetti. She dropped a generous spoonful of special cat food on each plate. For safe measure, she placed a small pile of cheese and crackers on a separate plate.

Before leaving, she said, "Squeekie, you're in charge as usual. Party to your hearts' content tonight. I'll be here early in the morning to clean up. Good night."

Squeekie watched for Robena to come out of the corner hole in the woodwork and quickly ran ahead to the party spread left by Michelle where the other cats were waiting. "Shhh, here she comes."

When Robena turned the corner around the end bookshelf, the cats yelled. "SURPRISE!"

"Oh yous guys! Yous gonna scares my babies."

"Are these your babies? They're so grown up already," Squeekie said.

"They's eyes is open and they's fur is comin' in. They's growin' fer sure. What's all dis; a party?"

"Robena, the newspaper credits the fire company for saving our store, but we know the whole truth. If not for your quick thinking and courage, we may have lost our happy home. We want to show you and your mouse friends our gratitude. All of us cats want you to have this as a thank-you for saving the bookstore."

Squeekie pushed a full bowl of dried cat food toward Robena.

"We each saved half our food this week for you and Michelle put all this here, too!"

"Whaaat?"

Robena quickly disappeared through the crack in the woodwork. She re-emerged from the hole minutes later, out of breath.

"Comes outs friends," she said.

The corner of the room was soon thick with mice as they streamed, one by one, from the little hole in the corner.

"Robena, you little pain in the butt! You know the rules. They cannot stay, this isn't a mouse motel. No chewing on the books and no poo pellets all over the place."

"I's remembers da rules, Squeek. Don't keeps tellin' me, you mangy meow machine."

Squeekie's lips curled, revealing his fangs as he jumped into the center of the crowd of mice, sending them running in every direction.

He chuckled as he strutted out of the room.

"Those are the rules, Robena. I want this cleaned up and all of them out of here by morning. Good night, you wretched mouse."

"Aww, goods nights my dear friend. I's loves you too, Squeek!"

Teddy Maurer

AUTHOR BIOGRAPHY

Teddy Maurer writes Sci-Fi and Fantasy stories. She is a member of Pennwriters and an alumni of A Novel Idea I and A Novel Idea II offered by the Perry County Council of the Arts. Her short story "Tera's Eyes" can be found in *Strange Magic* published by Sunbury Press, available on their website or on other online retailers. She lives in the Harrisburg, PA area with her furry assistant, Joey. Visit her Facebook page at https://www.facebook.com/TeddyMaurerAuthor/.

SQUEEKIE'S APPEARANCE RIDER

Jay Smith

Squeekie the Bookstore Cat™ is thrilled about the opportunity to share stories from his bestselling book "The Nine Lives of Squeekie the Bookstore Cat" at your event. Please keep in mind that Squeekie is happy to meet with members of the general public and sign copies of his books, but his time must be carefully managed to allow him a chance to relax and draw on creative energy for his many, important projects.

Squeekie the Bookstore Cat™ has enjoyed a meteoric rise to superstardom in the year since the release of his first book. Such a transition can take a toll on artists who must maintain control of their instrument in order to meet their many obligations. Your cooperation and support in this endeavor are appreciated.

This appearance rider is part of his appearance contract and the vendor or promoter (hereafter referred to as "client") is bound to make such accommodations for Squeekie the Bookstore Cat™ (hereafter referred to as Talent) prior to the event. Any substitutions or variations from this rider must be approved by Talent's representatives in writing 72 hours prior to any appearance.

    1. Police Protection. The Client will ensure the security of Talent by making available at least one security officer for every 100 anticipated visitors to the event. Each security officer must have a minimum of a first-degree black belt in a form of martial arts. And they must smile. And they must be nice. Until it is time to not be nice.

2. Charitable Contribution. A portion of the proceeds from each appearance must go to Castaway Critters, a charity that makes sure all of Talent's foster brothers and sisters find good forever homes.
3. Local Accommodations and Transportation. Talent will be housed in a "3-to-4-star" pet-friendly hotel the night and checking out the morning after the final appearance date. Talent will audition drivers the day of arrival and select who will shuttle him around and offer loving attention, pets, and scratches.
4. Talent will not share a table with other guests of the event. Talent will sit on each guest table for a moment to decide which is the best table.
5. Talent will visit every other table at the event at random and sit on it regardless of what is happening or what is on the table at that time.
6. Talent will not share billing or marketing with other guests. Talent will hold top billing.
7. Guests must be pre-approved for scratches, pets, and belly rubs. There will be no scratching of the hind quarters because that's just weird.
8. Comfy Naptime Bed. The Client will provide Talent with a memory foam cat bed for use between appearances.
9. Food and Drink. Client promises to provide, at no cost to Talent, 2 liters of uncarbonated spring water in a motorized water dish with an automatic recycling and filter system that maintains water temperature of 42 degrees. Client will also provide the motorized water bowl. Client will also provide a six-ounce bag of Gooshie's-brand seafood treats, presented in a shallow ceramic bowl. All green treats will be removed by hand.
10. All press access to Talent must be pre-approved by Talent's representative. "Cat Life" and "Feline Fancy" magazines are not to be granted press credentials due to their biased reporting of Talent's weight and singing voice. Talent will grant 30-second interviews to local outlets in a press room as time permits.

The Second and Third Nine Lives of Squeekie the Bookstore Cat

ABOUT THE AUTHOR

Squeekie was the bookstore cat at The Cupboard Maker Books in Enola, Pennsylvania. He loved treats, people, the foster cats that come through his store, and Annika. After living and loving at the bookstore for eight years, Squeekie passed away on March 24, 2021.

www.ingramcontent.com/pod-product-compliance
Lightning Source LLC
Chambersburg PA
CBHW071450080526
44587CB00014B/2055